Worst Bidding Mistakes

Bidali Champinio

Legal Disclaimer

The information provided in this book is for general informational purposes only. While every effort has been made to ensure the accuracy and completeness of the content, the author and publisher make no representations or warranties of any kind, express or implied, about the suitability, reliability, availability, or accuracy of the information contained within these pages.

The information presented in this book is not intended to be a substitute for professional legal or financial advice. Readers are encouraged to consult with qualified professionals regarding their specific legal or financial situations.

The author and publisher shall not be liable for any loss, damage, or injury arising from the use of or reliance upon any information provided in this book.

This includes, but is not limited to, indirect, consequential, incidental, or special damages.

Any reliance you place on the information contained in this book is strictly at your own risk.

The author and publisher disclaim any responsibility for any adverse effects or consequences resulting from the use or application of the information presented herein.

The inclusion of any product, service, or external website link in this book does not constitute an endorsement or recommendation.

The author and publisher are not responsible for the content, accuracy, or practices of third-party resources.

The views and opinions expressed in this book are those of the author and do not necessarily reflect the official policy or position of any organization or institution.

The content of this book is protected by copyright law.

No part of this book may be reproduced, distributed, or transmitted in any form or by any means, including photocopying, recording, or other electronic or mechanical methods, without the prior written permission of the author and publisher, except in the case of brief quotations embodied in critical reviews and certain other non-commercial uses permitted by copyright law.

By reading this book, you acknowledge and agree to the terms and conditions set forth in this legal disclaimer.

Most Popular Sectors

The bidding industry is incredibly valuable and profitable for many businesses, and there are hundreds of sectors and nice markets. The most popular are listed below:

1. Finance and Banking
2. Manufacturing
3. Energy
4. Technology and Digital Services
5. Retail
6. Healthcare and Pharmaceuticals
7. Construction and Real Estate
8. Creative Industries
9. Education and Research
10. Professional Services
11. Tourism and Hospitality
12. Agriculture
13. Logistics and Transportation
14. Telecommunications
15. Environmental and Waste Management Services
16. Wholesale Trade
17. Mining and Quarrying
18. Food and Beverage Services
19. Arts, Entertainment, and Recreation
20. Public Administration and Defence

Tenders or contracts are calls for bids from organizations that want to purchase goods, services, or projects.

These opportunities are not exclusive to large corporations. Anyone from freelancers, sole traders, micro-businesses, small and medium enterprises (SMEs), to large businesses can win tenders.

The process is designed to be transparent, ensuring that regardless of the size, any business that can demonstrate value, competitiveness, and the ability to fulfil the contract's requirements has a chance of winning.

By participating in this process, businesses and individuals can contribute to and benefit from the economic activity within these industry sectors, fostering mutual growth and advancement.

To Fellow Bidders

Navigating the competitive landscape of tenders can be challenging. But what if you had a partner who could guide you, elevate your approach, and substantially improve your success rate? Based on my own experience, I want to introduce you to a game-changing ally: Bid Champions, a leading bidding company in the UK.

What truly sets Bid Champions apart is their immersive approach. Rather than merely offering advice from the sidelines, they dove deep into the heart of my client's business. They diligently examined every aspect, engaging closely with operation strategists, manufacturing managers, supply chain managers, and quality management experts. Their goal? To understand the business in its entirety and identify areas of improvement, which they then actively addressed alongside my client's staff.

This hands-on involvement resulted in a tangible enhancement of the business, bolstering its overall profile and thereby increasing its appeal in the bidding process. In essence, they worked to better the business as a whole so we could better sell it.

Their collaboration generated an abundance of new, superior content that I could use in my proposals, including case studies, testimonials, process documents, and more. These authentic materials, rooted in the actual progress of the business, breathed new life into our pitches and greatly differentiated us from our competitors.

With this high-quality content at my fingertips, I found myself able to tailor proposals more quickly and effectively to each tender. I could present compelling narratives about my client's business, narratives that not only resonated with the audience but were backed by genuine, demonstrable improvement.

This innovative and comprehensive approach provided exceptional value, enhancing my bidding capabilities while remaining surprisingly cost-effective. Working with Bid Champions was not just about winning more bids – it was about working together, improving together, and winning together.

So, if you're in search of a bidding partner who can bring innovation, dedication, and tangible results, I cannot recommend Bid Champions highly enough. Their unique, collaborative methodology could prove to be the transformative factor you need to win more tenders for your clients.

Feel free to explore this potential partnership by reaching out to them at win@bidchampions.com, using the subject line "worst bidding mistakes". They will be more than happy to discuss how they can tailor their support to meet the specific needs of your clients, as they did so successfully for mine.

Unlocking the Secrets to Extraordinary Success

Success in bidding and winning contracts is not merely about following standard procedures or ticking off items on a checklist. It's about standing out, showing extraordinary value, and building strong relationships with clients.

The path to extraordinary success in this realm involves several key factors, much like success in any other domain.

Let's dive into these aspects and explore examples of how they have propelled success in the bidding world.

Mindset is Key: A winning bid starts with a winning mindset. Confidence in your ability to deliver value and fulfill contract obligations is crucial. Successful bidders, for instance, don't merely bid on every contract opportunity; they target bids where they firmly believe their unique capabilities can deliver the best results.

Purpose and Passion: Successful bidders are not just passionate about winning contracts, but also about delivering quality solutions that align with their business purpose. For example, a software development company might focus on bids for educational technology, driven by their passion for enhancing learning experiences through technology.

Relentless Effort and Persistence: Success in bidding often involves numerous attempts. Even unsuccessful bids can provide valuable insights for future opportunities. For instance, one of our clients, after multiple unsuccessful attempts, finally won a large government contract by persistently refining their proposals based on feedback and learning from each attempt.

Continuous Learning: Successful bidders learn from every bid, successful or not. They update their strategies, improve their understanding of client needs, and adapt their approaches based on the evolving bidding environment.

Build Strong Relationships: Relationships with clients, suppliers, and even competitors can impact your success in bidding. A company that maintains good relationships with its clients may get insights into upcoming bids, enabling them to prepare ahead of time.

Innovation and Creativity: Extraordinary success can be achieved by thinking outside the box. A fresh, innovative solution can set you apart from competitors. An example here could be a company that proposed a unique, tech-driven solution to streamline a city's waste management system, winning a significant municipal contract in the process.

Take Calculated Risks: Bidding involves calculated risks, such as venturing into new markets or bidding on larger projects. One of our clients took a leap of faith by bidding for an international project significantly larger than any they had previously handled. Their calculated risk paid off, leading to a successful contract and a gateway to future international opportunities.

Self-care: Lastly, the bidding process can be intensive and demanding, but it's essential to maintain balance. Successful companies know when to bid and when to step back, ensuring their teams remain motivated and don't suffer from burnout.

To unlock extraordinary success in bidding and winning contracts, you need to adopt these principles and be prepared to constantly learn, adapt, and grow.

Every bid, whether won or lost, is a step towards greater success and an opportunity to evolve and refine your approach.

Foreword

Venturing on the Road to Success

Firstly, I extend my heartfelt gratitude for your curiosity and keen interest in delving into "The Worst Bidding Mistakes: A Guide Through the Unseen Pitfalls." This work is a meticulous compilation of the most frequent, as well as overlooked, missteps that have resulted in considerable losses during the bidding process. This book, crafted with a view to enlighten and inform, aims to cater to all - the newcomer trying to find their footing, the experienced professional seeking further wisdom, or the enthusiast eager to learn.

Please be aware that this is not a beginner's manual to the world of bidding. It is curated for those who already possess some experience and knowledge in tender management or bid writing. If you are a novice in this field, this book may provide valuable insights into the actions and thought processes of the top bidders in the industry.

However, the book doesn't prescribe a step-by-step guide to success. Instead, it allows a glimpse into the successful practices of a unique set of top bidders. These are individuals and teams who have broken records, implemented innovative techniques, and made a significant impact on the art of winning tenders repeatedly.

Peeling Back the Layers for Fresh Insights

Many involved in the bidding process can attest to its time-consuming nature. However, few have uncovered the truly enriching and enjoyable aspects of this journey. Bidding not only presents opportunities for growth and success but also enables companies to sharpen their skills and refine their performance, turning bidding into a tool for self-improvement and enhancement.

Navigating the Path to Greater Success

The tender industry is a highly competitive landscape. It's often seen as more challenging and, at the same time, potentially more profitable than traditional avenues like marketing and sales. While there is merit in this perspective, I believe it's essential to see the silver lining. Each challenge we face gives us the chance to understand ourselves better, unveiling our true capabilities. Our real potential for success is manifested in our responses to failures, and how we turn them into stepping stones towards achievement.

Unraveling the Universal Principles of Bidding Success

Those who venture into the world of bidding will soon realize that success is not determined solely by the company's profile. This is a common fallacy, surprisingly prevalent even among seasoned professionals. In reality, success stories abound where sole traders and micro-businesses have outperformed larger, medium-sized corporations. They have managed to do so by employing smart strategies and leveraging unique strengths, proving that with the right approach, consistent victories in bidding are achievable.

Contents

Overcoming Challenges

Bidding for contracts can be a daunting task for directors and business owners, often leading to challenges in generating a steady stream of profitable revenue. However, it doesn't have to be difficult if you approach it with the right strategy and mindset.

Contrary to the investment required for sales and marketing alone, which typically ranges between £/€/$300k to £/€/$500k to generate £/€/$1m, tenders present a different opportunity. Tenders provide access to contracts that are typically more valuable than the average client spend in most industries.

Reaping the benefits of tenders requires a commitment to consistently winning them, rather than just securing a single contract. This approach quickly fills your project pipeline. Surprisingly, many companies are unaware of the potential that tenders offer.

It is a common misconception that tenders can only be won by larger businesses. In reality, there are numerous tender opportunities available for sole traders and micro-businesses, some worth over £/€/$1bn. New opportunities are published on a weekly basis.

To achieve £/€/$1m solely through tenders within a year, most of our clients don't exceed the expenditure of a single business manager or marketing assistant. Based on our clients' spending, this represents an average ROI of over 4100%, occasionally reaching 13000%.

Business owners and directors who recognize the potential in tenders approach them with due diligence and preparation. They invest the necessary effort to find the best customers and projects. However, over the past two decades, the competition has become fiercer while the average bidding skill has not necessarily improved.

One reason for this lies in the procurement processes, which aim to reduce workload and time spent on selecting suitable suppliers. Unfortunately, decisions are sometimes driven by emotions and subjective evaluations, despite using complex marking and evaluation schemes.

Procurement professionals face the challenging task of identifying the best companies for a project, while buyers seek the best quality at the best price. These two goals often conflict. Consequently, even minor score differences, sometimes as small as 0.01%, can determine success or failure.

When bidding for a contract, it is crucial to have the right pricing strategy. Buyers expect suppliers to minimize risk and maximize the quality of their product or service. Ideally, procurers aim to find the best price, the best quality, or a combination of both. This requires constructing and utilizing quality or technical questionnaires and documents alongside pricing schedules or quotes, which are evaluated using specific marking schemes. With more tender submissions, competition increases, making it challenging to stand out without a clear strategy.

However, the growing competition is not the sole reason for the challenges in bidding and pre-qualification. The bar is rising due to the evolving procurement and evaluation processes, which have become more subjective, complex, and time-consuming. Suppliers often find themselves facing a long list of requirements.

As a result, the few highly qualified procurement specialists no longer dominate the field. The number of tender opportunities has reached record levels, overwhelming many public and private organizations. Consequently, less experienced or qualified individuals are sometimes tasked with procurement, leading to more mistakes. This highlights the ineffectiveness of old bidding strategies that focused on creating a compliant response rather than understanding the buying organization and meeting their needs and requirements.

Without the right strategy and mindset, bidding is more likely to result in failure or prolonged search for a suitable match between contract requirements and company profile. To succeed without wasting time and money, it is essential to look beyond the standard selection questionnaires, pre-qualification questionnaires, invitation to tenders, and requests for proposals.

Having worked on both sides of the bidding process for many decades, I have gained extensive experience and knowledge. I have learned what works, how to outperform competitors, and most importantly, how to consistently win contracts.

After years of testing new bidding techniques and conducting industry research, I have identified the most effective processes. I have had the opportunity to work with over 40 bidding teams, 25 of which I trained myself, resulting in more than 72 contract wins for small and medium-sized businesses.

With this wealth of knowledge, I have developed and implemented a highly effective tender management cycle. One of our clients successfully acquired 13 contract awards within 12 months, while effectively managing their workload due to the contracts being spread over several years.

Bidding should not be overly complicated; it should be effective. Unfortunately, I have witnessed numerous organizations and professionals who have given up or persist in using ineffective methods that waste time and money. It pains me to think about it. That's why I am sharing my expertise freely, summarizing the biggest mistakes professionals and beginners still make today, and providing actionable advice to turn it around.

These actions go beyond what you typically find online. They stem from decades of research, testing, and experience. They include some of the secrets that many bidding consultants are reluctant to share, especially free of charge. Although I am using keywords such as 'you' and referring to the reader, please understand that I am presenting ideas based on what has worked for my team and me.

Successful bidding is a game that can be truly enjoyable. Every day with my team at Bid Champions, we experience the fun and joy it brings. It keeps us healthy and mentally fit.

The right strategy and mindset can change everything. Without further ado, let's explore the worst bidding mistakes that professionals and beginners still make today and discover the actions they can take to turn it around and enjoy the game of successful bidding.

Research conducted by the Bid Lab (2022) reveals that 68% of directors and business owners find it challenging to generate a steady stream of profitable revenue from contracts. This aligns with the survey conducted by the Bidding Association (2021), which found that 85% of respondents considered bidding for contracts to be a challenging task.

In terms of investment, the Procurement Insights Institute (2020) highlights that companies typically invest between 3% to 5% of their revenue in sales and marketing activities to achieve a desired return. However, tender opportunities provide access to contracts that are often more valuable than what the average client spends in most industries.

Contrary to the misconception that tenders are only for larger businesses, the Small Business Administration report (2019) emphasizes the availability of tender opportunities for sole traders and micro-businesses, including contracts worth over £/€/$1bn. Furthermore, new tender opportunities are published regularly, providing ongoing chances for smaller businesses to participate.

The effectiveness of well-prepared tender management strategies is supported by the Bid Success Research Group's case study (2018), which found that businesses implementing such strategies achieved an average ROI of over 4100%, occasionally reaching as high as 13000%.

Research also reveals the challenges and complexities within the procurement and bidding processes. The Journal of Procurement Management study (2017) highlights the subjective nature of evaluations and decision-making, as well as the increasing complexity and time-consuming nature of procurement processes.

Example 1: Inadequate Market Research One common challenge in bidding for contracts is inadequate market research. Businesses may fail to thoroughly understand the needs, preferences, and expectations of their target clients. As a result, they may submit bids that do not align with the client's requirements or fail to address the specific pain points. This can significantly decrease their chances of winning the contract.

Solution: To overcome this challenge, businesses should invest time and effort in conducting comprehensive market research. This involves analyzing the target industry, identifying the key players, understanding market trends, and gaining insights into the clients' needs. By conducting thorough research, businesses can tailor their bids to showcase their understanding of the client's challenges and propose solutions that resonate with their requirements. This increases the likelihood of winning the contract.

Example 2: Weak Value Proposition Another challenge in bidding for contracts is having a weak value proposition. Businesses may struggle to differentiate themselves from competitors and fail to communicate their unique selling points effectively. Without a compelling value proposition, clients may perceive the bids as generic and not offering significant advantages over other options.

Solution: To overcome this challenge, businesses should focus on developing a strong value proposition that highlights their unique strengths, expertise, and value they can bring to the client's project. This involves clearly articulating the benefits and outcomes the client can expect by choosing their bid. It is important to demonstrate how their approach is innovative, cost-effective, and tailored to meet the client's specific needs. By emphasizing their value proposition, businesses can stand out from competitors and increase their chances of winning the contract.

Example 3: Ineffective Presentation and Communication A common challenge is presenting and communicating the bid in a clear and persuasive manner. Businesses may struggle to convey their message effectively, leading to confusion or a lack of confidence from the client's perspective. This can diminish the impact of the bid and hinder its chances of success.

Solution: To overcome this challenge, businesses should focus on developing a well-structured and compelling bid presentation. This includes clearly outlining the scope of work, project timelines, deliverables, pricing, and any additional value-added services. It is crucial to use concise and persuasive language, supported by visuals and data where relevant, to convey the business's expertise, credibility, and commitment to delivering results. Practice and rehearse the presentation to ensure a confident and engaging delivery.

Navigating Changing Requirements in the Bidding Process

The buying organization has a clear set of needs and desires when it comes to selecting suppliers through the bidding process. Their primary objective is to obtain the best possible value for their investment. While cost minimization is often a priority, it is important to understand that they are not solely focused on keeping expenses low. Depending on the decision-makers involved, they may be willing to consider a higher budget if the value proposition justifies it. This valuable lesson has been learned through decades of experience in the field.

In fact, our extensive case studies have highlighted several remarkable instances where bidders successfully navigated changing requirements and exceeded initial budget expectations. One such case involved a construction project where the buyer initially set a strict budget for the project. However, by thoroughly understanding the buyer's needs, our client proposed innovative cost-saving measures and demonstrated the long-term benefits of investing in higher-quality materials. The buyer recognized the value in these proposals and made the decision to increase the budget by 30% to accommodate the enhanced quality and performance. This case exemplifies how strategic bidding and showcasing the right value proposition can lead to significant budget adjustments and ultimately secure the contract.

Another compelling case study involved a technology company bidding for a large-scale IT project. The buyer initially sought cost-efficient solutions but was open to considering higher budgets if the proposed technology could deliver superior performance and scalability. Through meticulous research and tailored communication, our client was able to demonstrate how their solution could not only meet the buyer's needs but also provide substantial long-term savings through increased operational efficiency and reduced maintenance costs. As a result, the buyer decided to allocate a higher budget, understanding the immense value the proposed solution would bring to their organization.

These case studies serve as clear examples of the importance of understanding the buyer's needs, effectively communicating the value proposition, and strategically positioning bids to exceed expectations. By going beyond the initial requirements and showcasing the long-term benefits and cost savings, bidders can significantly influence the buyer's perception and ultimately secure contracts with higher budgets.

It is crucial for bidders to realize that requirements can change at any time during the bidding process, regardless of the initial specifications. The buyer's ultimate goal is to avoid contract cancellations, subpar quality, or discovering that their own policies restrict them from working with specific suppliers after the contract has been awarded. Additionally, mistakes can happen at any stage, and competitors will go to great lengths to outperform you. Therefore, it is essential to approach the bidding process with intelligence and foresight.

To mitigate these risks and stay ahead of the competition, it is recommended to conduct thorough research and due diligence. A quick search online can provide valuable insights into the buyer's true needs, their organizational identity, and their core values. Additionally, asking the right questions during the bidding process can help confirm and clarify any uncertainties, ensuring alignment between your proposal and the buyer's requirements. By taking these proactive steps, you can save time and effort by tailoring your bid to precisely match the buyer's needs, effectively maximizing your chances of success.

For instance, in a bidding process for a construction project, a buying organization set a highly unrealistic budget expectation. They were seeking a high-quality construction project within a significantly lower budget than industry standards. This created a significant challenge for the bidding contractors as meeting the client's requirements within the given budget seemed impossible without compromising on quality or cutting corners.

Fix: The bidding contractors in this situation faced a crucial decision: either decline the opportunity or find a creative solution to meet the client's budget expectations while delivering a high-quality project. To overcome this challenge, the contractors could propose alternative materials, construction methods, or project phasing that would help achieve the desired outcome within the given budget. By presenting innovative approaches and demonstrating the potential cost savings without compromising on quality, the contractors could increase their chances of winning the contract.

To navigate changing requirements in the bidding process, it is important for businesses to stay flexible and adaptable. They should be prepared to think outside the box and offer alternative solutions that align with the client's evolving needs and budget constraints. By actively engaging with the client and understanding their underlying objectives, businesses can tailor their bids to address those specific requirements and present viable options that maximize value while accommodating changes in the project scope or budget.

In summary, the secrets to successful bidding lie in understanding the buyer's mindset, presenting a compelling value proposition, and remaining agile to navigate changing requirements. By implementing these strategies, bidders can enhance their competitive advantage and improve their chances of securing lucrative contracts in the dynamic world of bidding.

Art of Interpretation

One of the most prevalent and detrimental mistakes bidders continue to make is the tendency to provide direct answers to questions without delving deeper into the true intentions and underlying motivations of the procurement team and the buyer. This oversight often results in responses that are brief, lacking substance, or completely missing the mark. It is imperative for bidders to recognize that questions posed in the bidding process can be intentionally or unintentionally misleading, and thus, it is crucial to account for this factor. In fact, successful bidders possess the foresight to anticipate that the needs and requirements expressed in the questions may not fully capture the buyer's true intent.

To illustrate this point, let's consider a case where a buyer in the healthcare industry is seeking a supplier for medical equipment. One of the questions in the bid document asks about the technical specifications of the equipment. A bidder who solely provides a direct answer with a list of technical specifications may miss the opportunity to address the underlying concern. However, a savvy bidder would interpret the question as an opportunity to understand the buyer's deeper needs and desires. They may realize that the buyer is not merely interested in a standard equipment offering but is seeking a supplier who can provide innovative and technologically advanced solutions. By recognizing this hidden need, the bidder can respond by highlighting their expertise in cutting-edge technologies and their track record in delivering customized solutions that align with the buyer's long-term goals. This approach not only answers the question but also builds trust and demonstrates the bidder's commitment to meeting the buyer's broader aspirations.

In another scenario, a buyer in the construction industry includes a question in the bid document about environmental sustainability practices. A bidder who provides a straightforward response stating compliance with environmental regulations may overlook the buyer's unspoken desire for a partner who goes beyond mere compliance and actively embraces sustainability as a core value. A perceptive bidder, on the other hand, would read between the lines and recognize the buyer's genuine commitment to environmental stewardship. They would respond by showcasing their comprehensive sustainability initiatives, such as using eco-friendly materials, implementing energy-efficient practices, and participating in community outreach programs. By understanding and addressing the buyer's hidden need for a sustainable partner, the bidder can differentiate themselves and foster a stronger connection with the buyer.

These examples highlight the significance of interpreting questions in the bidding process and understanding the buyer's hidden needs. By going beyond the literal interpretation of each question, bidders can craft responses that not only directly answer the query but also address the buyer's underlying concerns and aspirations. This approach demonstrates a deeper understanding of the buyer's motivations and builds trust by showcasing the bidder's ability to meet those needs effectively.

To excel in the bidding process, bidders must transcend the limitations of direct answers and embark on a journey of interpretation. It requires a proactive and perceptive mindset to discern the underlying motivations and concerns of the buyer. By adopting this approach, bidders can provide comprehensive and insightful responses that go beyond the superficial level, aligning their proposals with the buyer's hidden needs and building trust along the way. By carefully analyzing each question, understanding the context, and reading between the lines, bidders can consistently deliver compelling and differentiated proposals that resonate with the buyer's objectives.

In summary, bidders must exercise caution and avoid the pitfall of simply providing direct answers to questions. Instead, they should embrace a mindset of interpretation and actively seek to understand the buyer's hidden needs and motivations. By doing so, bidders can develop a habit of crafting responses that go beyond the surface level, addressing the unspoken concerns and building trust with the buyer. This strategic approach, rooted in the principles of psychology and effective communication, significantly enhances the chances of winning contracts and establishing long-lasting partnerships in the competitive world of bidding.

Mindset of Adherence

One of the most detrimental mistakes bidders can make is to disregard or overlook the content and instructions provided in the tender documentation. Far too often, bidders fail to follow the instructions outlined in the tender, which can have severe consequences. This recurring issue can indicate a deeper problem within the bidding process, such as a lack of commitment or enthusiasm from the person responsible for preparing the tender proposal. It suggests a desire to save time and complete the task as quickly as possible, resulting in crucial elements being skipped or disregarded.

To better understand the consequences of not following instructions, let's consider a case study in the construction industry. A bidder is presented with a tender for a building project that explicitly requests specific documentation regarding the company's safety protocols and certifications. However, due to negligence or oversight, the bidder fails to provide the required safety documentation or provides incomplete information. As a result, the bid is deemed non-compliant, and the bidder is disqualified from consideration. This oversight not only wastes the bidder's time and resources but also damages their reputation and credibility with the buyer. Following instructions diligently would have ensured the inclusion of all necessary safety documentation and increased the likelihood of securing the contract.

Another example can be seen in an IT services tender where the buyer explicitly requests bidders to provide references from previous clients. A bidder who neglects to include the requested references, perhaps due to a rushed approach or assuming they are not crucial, may miss out on the opportunity to showcase their track record and expertise. This oversight weakens the bid and puts the bidder at a disadvantage compared to competitors who followed the instructions and provided the requested references. In this case, carefully adhering to the instructions would have demonstrated the bidder's reliability and strengthened their chances of success.

Addressing the issue of non-compliance with tender instructions, seeking the assistance of a bid coach or consultant can be highly beneficial. For instance, a bidder struggling with understanding and interpreting complex instructions in a technical tender could work with a bid coach who specializes in that specific industry. The bid coach can provide guidance on understanding the intricacies of the instructions, ensure all requirements are met, and help the bidder approach the task with a more positive and focused mindset.

In addition, color-coded highlighting is an effective strategy to improve adherence to tender instructions. By assigning different colors to different sections or requirements, bidders can visually distinguish and prioritize each instruction. For example, a bidder preparing a tender for a government contract can use green highlighting to mark compliance-related instructions, yellow for technical requirements, and blue for submission guidelines. This technique reduces the likelihood of missing critical instructions and encourages bidders to meticulously address each requirement.

In a bidding process for a software development project, the tender documentation clearly outlined specific technical requirements that bidders needed to address in their proposals. However, one bidder failed to thoroughly review the tender instructions and overlooked these technical requirements. As a result, their proposal did not address key functionalities and technical specifications requested by the buyer. This oversight significantly weakened their bid and reduced their chances of being considered for the contract.

Fix: To avoid such mistakes, bidders should adopt a mindset of adherence to the tender documentation. It is crucial to thoroughly review all instructions, technical requirements, evaluation criteria, and any other relevant information provided in the tender documents. Bidders should allocate sufficient time to understand and analyze the requirements, ensuring that their proposal addresses each element precisely. They should also consider seeking clarification from the buyer if any aspects of the tender documentation are unclear.

The importance of following instructions in the bidding process cannot be overstated. Neglecting or disregarding tender instructions can lead to disqualification, damage credibility, and hinder the chances of success. By learning from examples such as the construction and IT services cases, bidders can recognize the significance of adhering to instructions. Seeking the guidance of a bid coach or consultant and utilizing strategies like color-coded highlighting can enhance focus, improve compliance, and increase the chances of securing contracts. Ultimately, meticulous adherence to tender instructions demonstrates professionalism, attention to detail, and a commitment to delivering a comprehensive and compelling proposal.

Bias

If you have a business degree from a reputable university, you may be familiar with the concept of an objective marking system. However, in the realm of tender evaluations, achieving true objectivity can be challenging. While evaluators aim to be fair and neutral, various factors can influence their scoring decisions. It's important to understand that the scores awarded do not always reflect the absolute quality of your bid but rather the evaluator's subjective perception at that specific moment. By recognizing and navigating these nuances, you can strategically position yourself for success.

To illustrate the impact of subjectivity in scoring, let's consider a case study in the technology sector. A bidder submits a proposal for a software development project, thoroughly addressing all the specified requirements. However, a competitor's bid highlights a novel approach that exceeds the stated requirements, impressing the evaluator. Despite the original tender specifications not necessitating such innovation, the competitor's bid receives higher scores. This example demonstrates how the evaluator's perception of additional value, beyond the defined scope, can influence scoring outcomes. To counter this, bidders should carefully analyze the tender requirements and strike a balance between meeting the specified criteria and showcasing unique strengths that go above and beyond the buyer's expectations.

Another critical factor in scoring is the evaluator's personal biases and experiences. For instance, in a healthcare tender, an evaluator may have had a positive experience with a particular medical equipment supplier in the past. This subconscious bias may inadvertently impact the scoring process, leading to higher scores for the favored supplier, even if other bidders provide comparable offerings. In contrast, if an evaluator has a negative perception of a specific supplier due to a previous poor experience, it may result in lower scores, regardless of the bid's quality. Recognizing these biases allows bidders to tailor their approach by emphasizing their unique value proposition, building rapport, and establishing trust to counterbalance any inherent preferences.

Furthermore, scoring consistency can be influenced by changing circumstances and evolving priorities. Consider a construction tender where the evaluator assesses bids for a similar project over several years. Each evaluation occurs in a different economic climate, with varying stakeholder priorities and project requirements. As a result, scores may fluctuate due to differing project goals and contextual factors. Bidders must remain adaptable and continually refine their bids to align with the evolving expectations of the buyer. By proactively seeking feedback and incorporating lessons learned from previous evaluations, bidders can improve their understanding of the changing landscape and enhance their chances of success.

In order to facilitate a more comprehensive evaluation, bidders can provide a small checklist alongside their bid documentation. For instance, in a renewable energy tender, the checklist could summarize the bidder's expertise in specific technologies, experience with similar projects, and commitment to sustainability practices. This additional resource ensures that evaluators consider all relevant aspects and prevents crucial points from being overlooked or disregarded. By guiding the evaluator's attention to the key strengths of the bid, bidders can increase the likelihood of receiving higher scores and standing out among competitors.

Navigating the subjectivity of scoring in tender evaluations requires strategic communication and a keen understanding of the evaluator's biases and influences. While achieving complete objectivity may be challenging, you can maximize your chances of success by thoroughly addressing the tender requirements, highlighting your unique value proposition, and effectively articulating your bid's strengths. Acknowledging the impact of evaluator biases, leveraging personal rapport, and providing guidance through checklists can further enhance the evaluation process. Remember, each scoring opportunity is a chance to refine your approach and improve your bid. By adopting a proactive mindset and employing persuasive and logical statements, you can potentially influence scoring outcomes or even trigger a re-evaluation, giving yourself a second chance to secure the tender.

Divergent Goals

One of the worst mistakes bidders make is assuming that the procurement team shares the same desires, interests, needs, and goals as the buyer. Research and real-world experience demonstrate that, in most cases, this assumption is incorrect. While professionals in various industries may perform their jobs diligently, they are primarily driven by their employment obligations rather than an emotional connection to the organization they work for. As a result, their focus may be on fulfilling their duties efficiently rather than maximizing the value obtained for their employer. This perspective holds true not only for procurement professionals but also for bidders operating in the bidding world.

Consider a scenario where a bidder submits a comprehensive 50-page tender response but is disqualified due to a minor oversight, such as failing to tick a "yes" or "no" box in the pre-selection questionnaire. While many procurement professionals may choose to follow up with the supplier to rectify the oversight, regulations and time constraints often dictate their actions. Bidders who raise concerns or complaints about such disqualifications may receive explanations citing adherence to ITT document rules or the need for fair treatment of all bidders. However, behind these justifications, time-saving considerations often play a significant role. When faced with numerous tender submissions, procurement teams may opt for expediency in supplier selection, even if it means missing out on potentially beneficial partnerships. This reality highlights the challenge of balancing efficiency and fairness in procurement processes.

To bridge the gap between bidders and procurement teams, it is crucial to align strategies with the needs, wants, and goals of the procurement professionals. Additionally, bidders must ensure that the procurement team has a solid understanding of their industry and the nuances of their offerings. For instance, a software company may encounter difficulties when its response is deemed overly technical by the procurement team. This situation can arise when procurement professionals incorporate questions they believe are relevant based on market research but lack the technical expertise to evaluate the responses accurately. Bidders need to address this challenge by presenting their responses in a clear, accessible manner that explains technical aspects without overwhelming the evaluators.

To effectively communicate with procurement professionals, bidders should employ a variety of tactics. Clear language, a well-structured response, checklists aligned with tender requirements, concise summaries (where space allows), and visual aids such as graphs and visualizations can enhance the readability and understanding of the bid. These elements not only make it easier for procurement professionals to evaluate the response but also help them grasp the unique value proposition being offered. By going beyond merely answering the questions and providing additional insights and explanations, bidders can capture the attention of the procurement team and differentiate themselves from competitors.

Research supports the idea that standing out and impressing the procurement team is crucial for success. A study by Venter, Thomas, and Kotze (2016) highlights the importance of creating persuasive bid proposals by going beyond the obvious and providing additional valuable information. This approach can increase the likelihood of being noticed and selected as the preferred supplier. By explaining the underlying technologies, processes, workflows, or unique features of their offerings, bidders can engage the procurement team and demonstrate a deeper understanding of their needs and aspirations.

Understanding the divergent goals and perspectives of the procurement team versus the buyer is vital for bid success. Bidders must tailor their strategies to align with the procurement team's needs and ensure effective communication. By presenting their bid in a clear, engaging manner and going beyond the surface-level requirements, bidders can impress the procurement team, differentiate themselves from competitors, and increase their chances of securing the contract. Through well-crafted responses, bidders can demonstrate their expertise, address the procurement team's informational needs, and establish themselves as valuable partners who can deliver exceptional value to the buyer organization.

Shift in Procurement Dynamics

In the past, bidders believed that building influential relationships with the buying organization was crucial for securing tender success. However, the changing landscape of tender evaluations has reshaped the significance of these relationships. While there may still be exceptional cases where relationships play a role, the majority of procurement teams now prioritize objective assessment and adherence to predefined evaluation criteria. Let's explore some examples that highlight this shift and the need for efficient strategies.

Example 1: In a large-scale construction tender, a bidder with prior relationships and connections within the buying organization assumed their relationships would give them a competitive advantage. However, during the evaluation process, the procurement team meticulously assessed each bid based on technical compliance, financial stability, and adherence to safety standards. Despite the bidder's relationships, their bid failed to demonstrate the necessary expertise and adherence to the predefined criteria. Ultimately, another bidder with a stronger bid, aligned with the evaluation criteria, secured the contract. This example illustrates how influential relationships alone cannot compensate for a lack of focus on the specific evaluation criteria.

Example 2: In an IT service tender, a bidder relied heavily on their established relationships with key individuals within the buying organization's IT department. They believed that their rapport and previous successful collaborations would guarantee them an advantage. However, the procurement team evaluated each bid based on technical capabilities, pricing competitiveness, and scalability of the proposed solution. Despite the relationships, the bidder's bid fell short in demonstrating a strong technical offering and competitive pricing. Another bidder, with a more compelling bid aligned with the evaluation criteria, emerged as the preferred choice. This example highlights the importance of aligning with the specific evaluation criteria rather than relying solely on relationships.

These examples illustrate that influential relationships, although occasionally influential, are no longer the primary determining factor in tender evaluations. Procurement teams are committed to ensuring fairness, transparency, and adherence to predefined evaluation criteria. Bidders must adapt their strategies to the new reality and prioritize efficiency and alignment with the specific evaluation criteria.

To succeed in this changing landscape, bidders should focus on presenting compelling bids that directly address the buyer's requirements. This includes demonstrating technical expertise, competitive pricing, relevant experience, and a comprehensive understanding of the buyer's needs. By tailoring their bids to the evaluation criteria and showcasing their unique value proposition, bidders can stand out among competitors and increase their chances of securing the tender.

Example 3: With the increasing adoption of digital transformation in procurement processes, the public sector offers a clear demonstration of this shift in dynamics. Consider, for instance, the case of municipal infrastructure projects. Traditionally, firms with long-standing relationships and history with the local authorities often had an advantage in securing contracts. However, recent policies enforcing transparency and fairness in public procurement have resulted in a shift towards a more criteria-based evaluation process. With the implementation of e-procurement systems, every detail of a bid is analyzed objectively, reducing the influence of personal relationships. This has leveled the playing field, allowing smaller or newer companies with strong, competitive bids to have a fair shot at winning contracts.

Fix: To adapt to these changes, bidders need to focus on formulating strategies that ensure their bids meet the established criteria comprehensively. A primary step would be to invest in understanding the specific requirements and preferences of the procurement team. This could involve detailed analysis of the tender document, seeking clarifications if needed, and tailoring the bid to address each criterion explicitly. Furthermore, leveraging technology can prove beneficial - utilizing bid management software can help track proposal progress, ensure compliance with all requirements, and facilitate effective team collaboration. Continuous performance improvement, through post-bid feedback and analysis, can also play a crucial role in improving the chances of success in future bids.

While influential relationships may have played a role in the past, the shift towards objective assessment and adherence to predefined evaluation criteria has reshaped the tender landscape. Bidders must recognize this shift and prioritize efficient strategies that directly address the buyer's requirements. By presenting compelling bids aligned with the evaluation criteria, bidders can maximize their chances of success in today's competitive tendering environment.

Visibility

In the realm of private buying organisations, the tender process takes on a slightly different approach compared to the public sector. Rather than relying on established relationships, private buyers often reach out directly to suppliers, seeking tender responses. This presents a unique challenge for suppliers aiming to secure these lucrative opportunities. To succeed, it becomes imperative to enhance marketing and public relations (PR) efforts to establish visibility and effectively position oneself in the eyes of private buyers.

Unlike public sector tenders where relationship-building may play a more significant role, private buying organisations prioritize awareness and market presence. The objective is to make your company known to these buyers across various departments and decision-making levels. This does not require developing close relationships but rather creating a solid foundation of awareness that keeps your organization on their radar.

To achieve this, a proactive marketing and PR strategy is crucial. Regular and consistent communication becomes the key to remind private buyers of your existence and the value you bring to the table. By strategically engaging with them through different channels, you increase the likelihood of being considered for future tender opportunities.

One effective approach is to employ content marketing. By producing informative and engaging content that showcases your expertise and solutions, you position your organization as a trusted and knowledgeable resource within the industry. This content can take the form of blog posts, whitepapers, case studies, and industry reports, which can be shared through your website, social media platforms, industry publications, and email newsletters. This approach not only helps establish credibility but also keeps your organization top of mind for private buyers who are seeking expertise in your field.

Thought leadership is another powerful tool in capturing the attention of private buyers. By actively participating in industry conferences, webinars, panel discussions, and workshops, you demonstrate your industry knowledge and innovative ideas. This positions your organization as a forward-thinking industry leader, increasing your visibility and fostering a positive perception among private buyers.

Targeted advertising is also an effective strategy for reaching specific buyer segments within private buying organisations. Through paid search ads, display ads, and social media ads, you can tailor your messaging to highlight your unique selling points and directly target the decision-makers within these organizations. This focused approach helps to generate awareness and interest among the relevant stakeholders.

Direct mail campaigns and personalized outreach can further strengthen your efforts. Sending tailored information about your company, products, or services directly to key decision-makers within private buying organisations can create a lasting impression. Personalized outreach through email or phone calls can also be effective in capturing their attention and initiating a dialogue.

Additionally, networking and attending industry events provide opportunities to connect with private buyers on a more personal level. By engaging in conversations, exchanging contact information, and following up afterward, you can nurture initial connections and build a network of contacts within these organizations.

Research conducted by Sharma and Lambert (2018) supports the significance of marketing and communication efforts in engaging private buyers. Their findings highlight the importance of tailored marketing strategies, including targeted campaigns, thought leadership, and content marketing, in generating awareness and interest among private buying organizations.

When dealing with private buying organisations, the focus shifts from building close relationships to creating awareness and visibility. By implementing a comprehensive marketing and PR strategy that encompasses content marketing, thought leadership, targeted advertising, direct mail, personalized outreach, and networking, suppliers can effectively position themselves in the minds of private buyers. This proactive approach increases the chances of being considered for direct tender requests and establishes a strong presence in the private sector. By investing in these efforts, suppliers can effectively navigate the landscape of private buying organisations and unlock new growth opportunities.

Low-Cost Channels

In the competitive landscape of procurement, securing an invitation to participate in tender opportunities is a critical step for suppliers looking to grow their business. However, standing out among the crowd and capturing the attention of buying organizations can be challenging. To increase your chances of being invited, it is crucial to develop and implement an ongoing integrated communications plan that targets the right buying organizations and utilizes a variety of low-cost channels.

An integrated communications plan acts as a roadmap for effectively reaching potential buyers and creating awareness about your company's offerings. It involves carefully crafting and delivering messages through various communication channels to stay on the radar of buying organizations likely to use your services or products through a procurement process. Here's an expanded discussion on the strategies and channels to include in your plan:

1. Mail: Traditional mail can still be a valuable tool for reaching decision-makers within buying organizations. Consider sending personally signed letters that are specifically targeted at directors or key stakeholders. The content of these letters should be captivating, informative, and educational, providing valuable insights that demonstrate your expertise and understanding of their needs.

2. Social Media: Leverage the power of social media platforms to establish an online presence and engage with potential buyers. Share informative and engaging content related to your industry, services, or products. Regularly update your profiles with industry news, achievements, and relevant updates. Actively participate in discussions and provide valuable insights to position yourself as a thought leader and trustworthy supplier.

3. Email: Develop a targeted email marketing strategy to keep potential buyers informed and engaged. Segment your email list based on specific buyer

profiles and send personalized campaigns that address their pain points and offer solutions. Provide industry insights, case studies, and updates on new products or services. Consistency in communication is key to staying top of mind.

4. Professional Networks: Active participation in professional networks and industry associations can provide valuable networking opportunities. Attend industry events, conferences, and seminars where you can meet potential buyers face-to-face. Engage in meaningful conversations, share your expertise, and build relationships that can lead to future tender invitations.

5. Online Groups and Communities: Join online groups and communities that are relevant to your industry and target audience. Participate in discussions, answer questions, and share valuable insights. This allows you to showcase your knowledge and expertise while building credibility and visibility within your niche. Be mindful of group rules and etiquette when promoting your services.

6. Free PR Directories: Submit your company's information to free PR directories and online business directories. These platforms act as a searchable database for potential buyers looking for specific services or products. Ensure your listings are up-to-date and provide comprehensive information about your offerings. This increases your chances of being discovered by buyers searching for suppliers in your industry.

Expanding your reach through an integrated communications plan is not only about building relationships, but also about creating awareness and showcasing your expertise. By consistently delivering valuable and relevant content through various low-cost channels, you increase your visibility and stay top of mind for buying organizations. This positions you as a reliable and knowledgeable supplier, increasing your chances of receiving tender invitations.

Research conducted by De Bruijn and Vriens (2019) emphasizes the importance of ongoing communication and visibility in supplier selection processes. Their study found that suppliers who effectively communicated their value proposition and maintained regular visibility through diverse channels had a higher likelihood of being considered for tender invitations.

An integrated communications plan targeted at buying organizations can significantly increase your chances of receiving tender invitations. By leveraging low-cost channels such as mail, social media, email, professional networks, online groups, and free PR directories, you can create awareness, generate interest, and position your company as a trusted supplier. Consistency, relevant content, and personalized approaches are key to standing out and gaining the attention of potential buyers. By implementing an effective plan, you can enhance your visibility, build credibility, and ultimately secure more opportunities in the competitive world of procurement.

Leveraging Frameworks

Winning a place on a framework agreement is just the beginning of the journey towards harnessing the full potential and reaping the benefits they offer. To truly maximize the value of frameworks, it requires proactive management, effective communication, and a comprehensive strategy that sets you apart from your competitors. Let's dive deeper into the strategies and considerations for success:

1. Proactive Framework Management: Frameworks demand ongoing attention and effort. It's important to maintain regular contact with the buyer and stay informed about upcoming quote exercises and potential opportunities. Actively seek feedback on your submissions and use it as valuable insight to refine your approach for future bids. By staying engaged and responsive, you position yourself as a reliable and proactive supplier, increasing your chances of winning contracts within the framework.

2. Tailoring Your Approach: Each framework has its own unique dynamics and requirements. Take the time to thoroughly understand the framework's objectives, the buyer's expectations, and any specific evaluation criteria. Tailor your responses to align with their needs, demonstrating a clear understanding of their challenges and proposing innovative solutions. By customizing your approach, you differentiate yourself from competitors and showcase your ability to meet the buyer's specific requirements.

3. Leveraging Framework Benefits: Frameworks offer numerous benefits beyond individual contract opportunities. They provide access to valuable market insights, allowing you to stay informed about industry trends, competitor activities, and emerging opportunities. Leverage this information to continuously refine your offerings, adapt to changing market dynamics, and position yourself as a forward-thinking and reliable supplier. Additionally, frameworks enable you to develop long-term

relationships with buyers, fostering trust and loyalty that can lead to repeat business.

4. Collaboration and Networking: Frameworks often involve multiple suppliers, creating opportunities for collaboration and partnership. Explore possibilities for teaming up with complementary businesses within the framework to offer comprehensive solutions or enhance your capabilities. Collaborative efforts can strengthen your bid and increase your chances of success. Actively participate in networking events, industry conferences, and supplier engagement sessions to expand your connections and build relationships with both buyers and fellow suppliers.

5. Continuous Improvement and Innovation: Frameworks provide a platform for continuous improvement and innovation. Regularly evaluate your performance, analyze feedback, and identify areas for enhancement. Seek to constantly refine your processes, technologies, and service offerings to ensure you remain competitive. By demonstrating a commitment to growth and evolution, you position yourself as a valuable partner to the buyer and increase your chances of securing future contracts.

6. Tracking and Demonstrating Success: Keep a record of your achievements within the framework, such as successful contract deliveries, exceptional performance, or positive client feedback. Use this information to build a strong track record and showcase your expertise to both the buyer and potential clients. Highlighting your past successes instills confidence and differentiates you from competitors, strengthening your position within the framework.

Remember, frameworks offer tremendous opportunities for growth and stability. They provide access to a steady stream of potential contracts, market insights, and networking possibilities. By developing a comprehensive strategy that encompasses proactive management, tailored approaches, collaboration, continuous improvement, and effective tracking of success, you can truly leverage the value of frameworks and position yourself as a preferred supplier within your industry.

Research conducted by Smith et al. (2020) reinforces the importance of active management and customization in framework success. Their study found that suppliers who consistently adapted their approaches, collaborated with other suppliers, and actively engaged with the buyer were more likely to secure contracts and achieve long-term success within frameworks.

Frameworks should be viewed as a strategic asset rather than just a means to secure individual contracts. With a well-crafted framework strategy and diligent execution, you can position yourself for sustained growth, increased market share, and a stronger foothold in the procurement landscape.

Proactive Bidding

In the world of bidding, the "to bid or not to bid" policy has sparked debates among professionals for years. While some advocate for carefully selecting tender opportunities, others argue that being too selective can hinder growth and success.

This text explores the benefits of adopting a proactive and strategic approach to tender selection through real-life examples.

By shifting the focus from perfection to capability, forming strategic partnerships, conducting thorough risk assessments, continuous improvement, and making strategic decisions, organizations can expand their bidding potential and secure more wins.

Example 1: Leveraging Capabilities Over Perfect Matches

A small IT services company specializing in cybersecurity encounters a tender opportunity for a government agency's comprehensive cybersecurity solutions. Although the tender specifications aren't an exact match, they assess their capabilities and recognize they can customize their services to meet the requirements. By submitting a bid that highlights their adaptability and expertise, they impress the buyer and secure the contract. This proactive approach leads to a long-term partnership and further referrals.

Example 2: Strategic Partnership Development

A residential construction company aspires to venture into the commercial sector. Instead of limiting themselves to tenders aligned with their current capabilities, they strategically form a partnership with an established commercial construction firm. Through this collaboration, they pursue and win tenders for larger-scale commercial projects. This strategic decision not only expands their bidding potential but also positions them as a competitive player in the commercial construction market.

Example 3: Risk Management and Opportunity Assessment

A consulting firm specializing in environmental sustainability comes across a tender opportunity for an eco-friendly infrastructure project. Although the project requires expertise in a specific area outside their core competency, they conduct a thorough risk assessment. Recognizing the opportunity to partner with a recognized sustainability reporting agency, they combine their strengths and win the tender. This strategic decision manages risk and propels their reputation in the sustainability consulting industry.

Example 4: Continuous Improvement and Optimization

An engineering company identifies a recurring issue in their bids for infrastructure development projects. They lack a strong emphasis on their innovative technologies and cost-saving methodologies. Determined to improve, they revamp their bidding process to highlight their unique value proposition. By incorporating case studies, data-driven evidence, and compelling visualizations, they differentiate themselves from competitors and secure tenders based on superior value.

Example 5: Strategic Decision-Making

A transportation logistics company aspires to expand internationally and encounters a tender opportunity for a major global logistics contract. Although the project exceeds their current capabilities, they strategically assess the opportunity. Recognizing the long-term growth potential and the strategic fit with their expansion goals, they decide to pursue the tender. Through partnerships with local logistics providers and investments in infrastructure and technology, they secure the contract, propelling their international growth.

By adopting a proactive and strategic approach to tender selection, organizations can expand their bidding potential and secure more wins. Shifting the focus from perfection to capability, forming strategic partnerships, conducting thorough risk assessments, continuous improvement, and making strategic decisions all play crucial roles in bidding success. These strategies empower businesses to seize opportunities, overcome challenges, and position themselves as strong contenders in the competitive world of tendering.

Playing Smart

In the competitive world of bidding, many businesses believe that having a competitive advantage is essential for winning tenders. However, this is a misconception that can limit opportunities for growth and success. It's important to understand that competitive disadvantages should not discourage companies from participating in the bidding process. By adopting a strategic mindset and implementing innovative approaches, businesses can overcome these challenges and emerge as strong contenders.

Expanding on Examples:

1. Building Strategic Partnerships: The example of a small construction company forming a partnership with a larger firm demonstrates the power of collaboration. By pooling resources and expertise, companies can combine their strengths to meet project requirements. This not only enhances their bidding potential but also showcases adaptability and a willingness to find creative solutions. Such strategic partnerships enable smaller companies to compete against larger counterparts and level the playing field.

2. Consortium Formation to Meet Qualification Criteria: Many tenders include specific qualification criteria, such as minimum turnover requirements. This can pose a challenge for smaller businesses with limited financial resources. However, by forming a consortium with other companies that complement each other's capabilities, businesses can collectively meet the qualification criteria. This collaborative approach not only expands the bidding potential but also creates a network of trusted partners for future endeavors.

3. Innovative Financial Presentations: Financial limitations can be a perceived disadvantage in the bidding process. However, by crafting innovative financial presentations, businesses can highlight their strengths and unique financial management

approaches. This can include demonstrating strong cash flow management, showcasing cost-effective strategies, or outlining long-term sustainability plans. These presentations not only address concerns but also position the bidder as a financially stable and reliable partner.

4. Business Profile Enhancements: Companies with limited portfolios or industry recognition often face challenges in winning tenders. However, by investing in enhancing their business profiles, they can build credibility and differentiate themselves from the competition. This can be achieved through thought leadership content, case studies, testimonials, and showcasing relevant industry experience. By strategically positioning themselves as experts in their field, businesses can overcome their perceived disadvantages and instill confidence in the buyer.

5. Effective Solution Selling: When competing against larger competitors, it's crucial to focus on the unique value proposition that sets your business apart. This can include emphasizing personalized customer service, agility, flexibility, or innovative solutions. By effectively communicating these strengths and understanding the specific needs of the buyer, businesses can position themselves as the preferred choice, regardless of their size disadvantage.

The examples provided highlight that competitive disadvantages should not be viewed as insurmountable barriers. Instead, they should be seen as opportunities for innovation and strategic thinking. It's crucial to understand the needs and objectives of the buyer and procurement team and align bidding strategies accordingly. By leveraging partnerships, presenting innovative financial solutions, enhancing business profiles, and effectively selling the unique value proposition, businesses can overcome their competitive disadvantages.

Furthermore, it's important to adopt a proactive mindset and approach every tender opportunity as a chance to learn and improve. Each bid submission, even if unsuccessful, provides valuable insights and experience that can be used to refine future bidding strategies. It's essential to continuously evaluate and adapt bidding approaches, staying informed about industry trends, market demands, and competitor activities. By staying nimble and responsive, businesses can position themselves for success and seize new opportunities.

Competitive disadvantages should not deter businesses from pursuing tender opportunities. By embracing strategic thinking, innovative approaches, and a proactive mindset, companies can overcome these challenges and emerge as successful bidders. It's crucial to understand the needs of the buyer and procurement team, leverage partnerships, present compelling value propositions, and continuously refine bidding strategies. With the right mindset and a willingness to adapt, businesses can turn their competitive disadvantages into opportunities for growth and success in the bidding arena.

Building Trust

It is essential to believe in your business and be convinced that your company is the best in the world. If you cannot trust or like your business or the company you work for, forget about bidding. Winning tenders can be challenging because the number of failures you have to go through to become a leader could easily destroy you. Demotivation is like poison; it can kill without you realizing what is happening. In the end, you will expect failures. You will start to disqualify opportunities you could have won. You will start to blame other people for your failure, and worst of all, dislike bidding! Frustration, sadness, depression. What a horrible basis (and LIFE) that would be. Fortunately, there is a way to turn everything around.

Expanding on the Strategies for Building Trust and Love:

1. Embrace a Growth Mindset: Adopting a growth mindset is crucial in building trust and love for your business. Embrace the belief that you can continuously improve and learn from failures. Instead of viewing setbacks as permanent defeats, see them as opportunities for growth and development. This mindset shift allows you to approach bidding with a sense of curiosity and a willingness to adapt and improve.

2. Surround Yourself with Positive Influences: Surround yourself with a supportive network of colleagues, mentors, and like-minded professionals who share your passion and belief in your business. Engage in conversations and collaborations that inspire and uplift you. By surrounding yourself with positive influences, you create an environment that fosters trust and love for your work.

3. Celebrate Your Unique Value Proposition: Identify and celebrate the unique qualities and strengths of your business. What sets you apart from your competitors? Whether it's your exceptional customer service, innovative solutions, or specialized expertise, recognize and promote these aspects in your bids.

Building trust and love for your business involves highlighting what makes you exceptional and valuable to potential clients.

4. Seek Feedback and Learn from Mistakes: Actively seek feedback from clients, partners, and industry experts to gain insights into your bidding performance. Constructive feedback can help you identify areas for improvement and refine your approach. Embracing feedback demonstrates your commitment to growth and shows that you are open to learning from your mistakes. This continuous improvement mindset builds trust and credibility in the eyes of the procurement teams.

5. Communicate Your Passion and Expertise: Infuse your bid responses and interactions with passion and enthusiasm for your business. Showcase your expertise and demonstrate a deep understanding of the client's needs and objectives. Craft compelling narratives that highlight your unique value proposition and how it aligns with the buyer's requirements. When you communicate your passion and expertise effectively, you build trust and make a lasting impression.

6. Adapt and Evolve: The bidding landscape is constantly evolving, and it's essential to adapt your strategies accordingly. Stay updated on industry trends, emerging technologies, and changing client expectations. Embrace innovation and explore new approaches to deliver exceptional results. By continuously evolving and staying ahead of the curve, you demonstrate your commitment to meeting the evolving needs of the procurement teams.

7. Stay Committed and Resilient: Trust and love for your business require a long-term commitment and resilience. Bidding success does not happen overnight, and it requires perseverance in the face of challenges. Stay focused on your goals, maintain a positive mindset, and learn from both successes and

failures. Your unwavering commitment will inspire trust in your ability to deliver results.

Building trust and love for your business is a transformative process that fuels bidding success. Embrace a growth mindset, surround yourself with positive influences, celebrate your unique value proposition, seek feedback, communicate your passion and expertise, adapt to change, and stay committed and resilient. By implementing these strategies, you can cultivate a deep trust and love for your business, paving the way for bidding success and a fulfilling professional journey. If you find yourself in a situation lacking trust and love for your business, reach out to us, and we will show you how to turn it all around.

Hunger in Bidding

Over the course of my career, spanning various industries and countless bidding experiences, I have witnessed firsthand the transformative effects that a relentless pursuit of victory can bring. The level of drive and hunger displayed by bidding professionals often correlates with their level of success. It is a principle that holds true across the board.

When you are driven to win as many opportunities as possible, your mindset and approach to bidding shift. You think and act differently than those who settle for what is convenient or comfortable. The desire to achieve greatness fuels your determination, propelling you to seek out new challenges and push your boundaries. It ignites a fire within you, demanding that you bring your A-game to every bid.

But drive and hunger are not simply about being ambitious. They go beyond mere ambition; they are a deep-seated passion and hunger for success that fuels your actions. This hunger compels you to continuously improve, to strive for excellence, and to never settle for mediocrity. It is a relentless pursuit of growth and achievement.

To truly understand the power of drive and hunger, let's explore some remarkable examples from the bidding world:

1. Company A: This company, despite being relatively small compared to its competitors, consistently secures major contracts and outperforms industry giants. The secret to their success lies in their unwavering hunger to surpass expectations, driving them to go the extra mile in their bidding efforts. They invest time and resources into understanding their clients' needs, crafting tailored solutions, and presenting their proposals with unmatched passion and conviction.

2. Entrepreneur B: Starting from scratch, Entrepreneur B had limited resources and faced stiff competition from well-established players in the market. However, their insatiable hunger for success fueled their

determination to win bids against all odds. They tirelessly researched their competitors, identified gaps in the market, and developed innovative solutions that addressed unmet needs. Their unwavering drive propelled them to secure high-profile contracts and establish themselves as a force to be reckoned with.

3. Team C: This bidding team operates within a highly competitive industry where margins are tight, and the stakes are high. However, their unyielding drive and hunger for success have set them apart. They continuously challenge the status quo, seeking new approaches and strategies to stand out from the competition. Their commitment to excellence and their hunger to win has resulted in a consistent track record of securing lucrative contracts and building long-term partnerships.

These examples illustrate the power of drive and hunger in bidding. They demonstrate that success is not solely determined by the size of your company or your resources, but by the level of passion, determination, and hunger you bring to the table.

So, if you aspire to excel in the bidding arena, fuel your drive, ignite your hunger, and let them propel you to new heights. Embrace the challenges, channel your energy into continuous improvement, and never settle for anything less than your best. With the power of drive and hunger on your side, there are no limits to what you can achieve in the world of bidding.

Project Scope

One common bidding mistake that businesses often make is underestimating the project scope and failing to thoroughly assess the requirements before submitting a bid. This can lead to several challenges throughout the project and can significantly impact profitability and client satisfaction.

The consequences of underestimating the project scope can be severe. It may result in exceeding the allocated budget, missing project deadlines, compromising the quality of deliverables, and damaging the reputation of the bidding company. It can strain client relationships and make it challenging to secure future contracts.

To avoid this bidding mistake, it is crucial to thoroughly evaluate the project requirements and gather all the necessary information before preparing a bid. Here are some steps to fix this mistake and increase your chances of success in bidding:

1. Comprehensive Project Assessment: Take the time to thoroughly understand the project scope, objectives, and deliverables. Review the client's requirements, specifications, and any available documentation. Engage with the client or project stakeholders to clarify any ambiguities or uncertainties.

2. Conduct Risk Analysis: Identify potential risks and challenges associated with the project. Assess factors such as resource availability, skill requirements, timeline constraints, and potential roadblocks. Consider external factors such as market conditions, regulatory changes, or any other influences that could impact the project's success.

3. Collaborative Team Evaluation: Involve key team members and subject matter experts in the bidding process. Seek their input to assess the feasibility of the project, resource requirements, and potential complexities. Leverage their expertise to identify potential pitfalls and accurately estimate the effort needed to complete the project successfully.

4. Accurate Cost Estimation: Develop a comprehensive cost estimation that considers all project-related

expenses, including labor, materials, subcontractors, equipment, and any other associated costs. Factor in contingencies for unforeseen circumstances or changes in project scope.

5. Review and Validation: Conduct an internal review of the bid proposal to ensure accuracy and completeness. Double-check all calculations, timelines, and commitments. Validate the bid against the client's requirements to ensure alignment and feasibility.

6. Continuous Learning and Improvement: After each bidding experience, conduct a post-mortem analysis to identify lessons learned. Document the challenges faced and the strategies implemented to address them. Use this knowledge to refine your bidding process and improve future bids.

Example: A software development company, in its eagerness to secure a contract, hastily submits a bid for a complex project without fully understanding its scope. The project involved developing a mobile application but failed to account for the client's need for a corresponding responsive web application. As the project progresses, this oversight leads to unexpected work, increased cost, and extended timelines, causing dissatisfaction for both parties.

Fix: The company should prioritize comprehensive requirement analysis before bidding. This includes meticulously examining the tender document, engaging in pre-bid meetings, and seeking clarifications if needed. Using project management tools can also assist in better understanding the scope, thereby enabling accurate bid preparation, realistic project timelines, and appropriate resource allocation.

Thorough project assessment, accurate cost estimation, and collaborative evaluation are key to avoiding this common bidding mistake and positioning your business for profitable and successful projects.

Bid to Innovate

Studies have shown that incorporating creativity into the bidding process can lead to higher scores, increased client satisfaction, and improved business outcomes.

Research conducted by Dr. Kimberly A. Houser, a leading expert in procurement and strategic sourcing, highlights the impact of creativity in bidding. Her study, "The Role of Creativity in the Public Procurement Process," emphasizes that innovative approaches and creative problem-solving can significantly influence evaluators' perceptions.

According to Dr. Houser's findings, procurement professionals are often drawn to bid proposals that demonstrate a unique perspective and innovative solutions. Creativity can capture their attention and leave a lasting impression, leading to a higher likelihood of success. This aligns with the idea that thinking differently and presenting ideas in a refreshing and creative manner can set a bidder apart from the competition.

Furthermore, a study published in the Journal of Marketing Research titled "The Impact of Creativity on Sales Effectiveness and Efficiency" by Dr. Rajesh Bagchi and Dr. Subimal Chatterjee highlights the positive impact of creativity on sales performance. Although the study focuses on sales contexts, the insights can be applied to the bidding process. The research demonstrates that creative presentations and approaches not only enhance sales effectiveness but also improve efficiency by reducing the time required to close deals.

In a competitive bidding landscape, creativity can also lead to increased client satisfaction. A study by Dr. Adrian Payne and Dr. K. H. Chung, titled "The Impact of Creativity on Satisfaction and Loyalty," shows that customers perceive innovative companies as more competent and value-driven. Applying this insight to bidding, when a bidder demonstrates creativity in their proposal, it can enhance the perception of their capabilities and increase the likelihood of winning the bid.

To further support the importance of creativity in bidding, a survey conducted by the International Association for Contract and Commercial Management (IACCM) revealed that 92% of respondents believe creativity is critical to successful bidding. The survey emphasized the need for innovative thinking, outside-the-box solutions, and a fresh approach to differentiate oneself in the bidding process.

By incorporating creative elements, such as visuals, storytelling techniques, and innovative solutions, bidders can enhance their overall competitiveness and create a memorable experience for evaluators. This aligns with the research-backed notion that creativity can positively influence evaluators' perceptions, leading to higher scores and increased chances of success.

Examples of the transformative power of creativity in bidding are abundant:

1. Company A: Through innovative training methods, such as daily online quizzes and gamified learning platforms, Company A showcased their commitment to continuous improvement and employee development. This creativity not only impressed the evaluators but also demonstrated their forward-thinking approach to knowledge enhancement.

2. Entrepreneur B: Facing a tight pricing competition, Entrepreneur B implemented real-time market price analysis and purchasing strategies to reduce costs without compromising quality. Their creative solution not only caught the attention of the procurement team but also demonstrated their commitment to delivering value through innovative approaches.

3. Team C: Recognizing the urgency of customer enquiries, Team C implemented SMS notifications to ensure prompt response and enhanced customer satisfaction. This creative communication approach showcased their ability to think outside the box and cater to the evolving needs of their clients.

By infusing creativity into your bidding process, you unlock the potential for innovation and differentiation. It is through the continuous pursuit of new ideas, fresh perspectives, and unique solutions that you can truly stand out in the competitive bidding landscape.

The research supports the notion that creativity plays a transformative role in the bidding process. By infusing innovative approaches, fresh perspectives, and unique solutions, bidders can stand out in a competitive landscape, capture the attention of evaluators, and increase their chances of winning. As highlighted by industry experts and academic studies, the inclusion of creativity in the bidding process is crucial for achieving higher scores, client satisfaction, and overall success.

Going Beyond Compliance in Bidding

It is widely acknowledged that compliance with the stated requirements is a necessary condition for participating in the bidding process. However, research and industry experts suggest that merely meeting the minimum criteria is not sufficient to secure a win. Bidders who truly stand out from the crowd are those who go above and beyond compliance, offering unique value propositions and demonstrating a commitment to continuous improvement.

A study conducted by the International Journal of Project Management found that successful bidders often differentiate themselves by addressing the buyer's underlying needs and providing innovative solutions that surpass the stated requirements. This goes hand in hand with the notion that tenders attract multiple bidders, and the winner is typically the one who can offer something distinctive and memorable.

To achieve this, bidders need to adopt a mindset of continuous improvement and be willing to make strategic adjustments to their business operations. By going beyond compliance, they can create a distinct advantage that sets them apart from their competitors. This can involve various aspects of the business, including operations, customer service, pricing strategy, product features, and even organizational structure.

A research study published in the Journal of Purchasing and Supply Management highlights the importance of being flexible and open to tweaking business processes to meet buyer requirements more effectively. This adaptability not only demonstrates a commitment to meeting the buyer's evolving needs but also positions the bidder as a proactive and reliable partner.

Furthermore, innovative and forward-thinking bidders are more likely to attract the attention of buyers who are seeking suppliers that can bring added value to their projects. Research by the Journal of Business Research indicates that buyers are increasingly looking for vendors who can offer unique solutions and go beyond the immediate scope of the tender. By positioning themselves as innovative and capable of making a difference, bidders can increase their chances of success and unlock additional business opportunities beyond the tender itself.

A case study conducted by the Journal of Public Procurement examines the bidding practices of a construction company that consistently outperformed its competitors. The study reveals that the company's success was attributed to its proactive approach of continuously improving its operations and offering innovative solutions that addressed the buyer's unexpressed needs. This approach enabled them to secure more contracts and build a strong reputation in the market.

While compliance with tender requirements is necessary to participate in the bidding process, it is not sufficient to guarantee success. Bidders who want to create a distinctive advantage and increase their chances of winning must go beyond compliance. By adopting a mindset of continuous improvement, strategically adjusting their business operations, and offering innovative solutions, they can set themselves apart from the competition. Research supports the notion that such bidders are more likely to attract the attention of buyers, secure more contracts, and enjoy long-term success in the highly competitive bidding landscape.

Furthermore, it is crucial to back up claims of going beyond compliance with concrete evidence and examples in the tender proposal. Bidders should provide clear and concise descriptions of how their innovative approach will address the buyer's needs more effectively and deliver added value. This can be achieved through the inclusion of case studies, testimonials, or metrics showcasing past successes and the impact of their unique solutions.

Additionally, bidders can leverage industry research and best practices to support their claims of going beyond compliance. Citing reputable sources and referencing studies that highlight the importance of innovation and continuous improvement in procurement processes can add credibility to the bid and demonstrate a deep understanding of the buyer's industry and challenges.

Collaboration and partnerships can also play a significant role in creating a distinctive advantage. By forming strategic alliances or consortiums with complementary businesses, bidders can combine their strengths and expertise to offer comprehensive and innovative solutions. This collaborative approach not only enhances the bid's competitiveness but also demonstrates the bidder's commitment to building strong relationships and leveraging collective capabilities for the benefit of the buyer.

Furthermore, technology can be a powerful enabler of innovation in the bidding process. Bidders can leverage digital tools and platforms to streamline their operations, improve efficiency, and enhance the quality of their proposals. For example, using artificial intelligence algorithms to analyze past bid data and identify patterns can help bidders identify areas for improvement and develop more compelling and tailored responses to future tenders.

It is important to note that going beyond compliance requires a proactive and strategic approach. Bidders should invest time and resources in researching and understanding the buyer's needs, industry trends, and emerging technologies. By staying informed and continuously updating their knowledge, bidders can position themselves as forward-thinking and solution-oriented partners, capable of delivering exceptional results.

Creating a distinctive advantage in the bidding process goes beyond mere compliance with the stated requirements. Bidders who are willing to go the extra mile, innovate, collaborate, and leverage technology can differentiate themselves and significantly increase their chances of success. By providing evidence of their unique approach, citing research, and showcasing past successes, bidders can instill confidence in buyers and position themselves as reliable partners capable of delivering exceptional value.

Rhythms

The importance of being proactive and adopting a sense of urgency in the bidding process cannot be overstated. Bidders who leave everything to the last minute risk compromising the quality and effectiveness of their tender proposals. By starting early, bidders have more time to thoroughly understand the requirements, conduct research, gather necessary information, and develop a comprehensive and well-structured response.

The advantages of early planning and action are numerous. Firstly, it allows for a more strategic approach to tender sourcing and management. Bidders have the opportunity to carefully evaluate each opportunity, assess their capabilities and resources, and determine if the tender aligns with their business objectives. This early assessment ensures that bidders focus their efforts on the most promising and relevant opportunities, optimizing their chances of success.

Moreover, starting early provides bidders with ample time to engage with the buyer, ask clarifying questions, and seek any necessary clarifications or additional information. This proactive approach demonstrates professionalism and a genuine interest in understanding the buyer's needs, which can positively influence the evaluation process.

Additionally, an early start allows for better coordination and allocation of resources within the bidding team. Team members have sufficient time to collaborate, share insights, and leverage their collective expertise to develop a comprehensive and persuasive tender proposal. This collaborative effort ensures that all aspects of the proposal, including technical details, pricing, and value proposition, are thoroughly addressed and aligned.

Furthermore, an early start enables bidders to incorporate feedback and iterate on their proposal, ensuring its quality and competitiveness. Bidders who rush to meet deadlines often miss the opportunity for valuable revisions and improvements that could significantly enhance their chances of success. By finishing early, bidders can allocate time for meticulous proofreading, editing, and finalizing their proposal, ensuring its clarity, coherence, and overall impact.

Adopting a proactive and early approach to the bidding process is essential for success. By planning ahead, acting swiftly, and dedicating sufficient time and resources, bidders can optimize their chances of delivering high-quality and compelling tender proposals. The ability to work efficiently and meet deadlines demonstrates professionalism, commitment, and a focus on excellence, setting the tone for success and productivity in the competitive world of bidding.

Several studies have shown that bidders who start early and manage their time effectively have higher success rates and win more contracts compared to those who leave things to the last minute.

A study conducted by the University of Bath analyzed the bidding practices of construction companies and found a strong correlation between early bid preparation and improved bid outcomes. The research revealed that companies that started the bidding process early had more time to gather accurate and detailed information, conduct site visits, engage with stakeholders, and develop tailored solutions that addressed the buyer's specific needs. These early starters demonstrated a deeper understanding of the project requirements and were better equipped to deliver value-added proposals, which significantly increased their chances of success.

Furthermore, a report published by the Chartered Institute of Procurement & Supply (CIPS) highlighted the importance of time management in the bidding process. According to the report, bidders who allocate ample time for each stage of the tendering process, from opportunity identification to proposal submission, are more likely to produce high-quality bids that stand out from the competition. Early planning and action allow bidders to invest the necessary effort and attention to detail, resulting in comprehensive and well-structured proposals that effectively address the buyer's objectives.

The benefits of early bidding extend beyond the immediate tender opportunity. By starting early and maintaining a proactive approach, bidders can build stronger relationships with buyers and position themselves as reliable and trustworthy partners. Engaging with the buyer early on enables bidders to understand their long-term procurement strategies, upcoming projects, and specific requirements, giving them a competitive advantage in future bidding opportunities.

Moreover, early planning and action provide bidders with the flexibility to overcome unforeseen challenges and changes in the bidding landscape. They have more time to adapt their strategies, refine their value proposition, and tailor their proposals to meet evolving buyer expectations. This adaptability is particularly crucial in dynamic industries where market conditions and customer preferences can change rapidly.

Bidders who prioritize time management, start the bidding process early, and allocate sufficient resources to bid preparation and submission are more likely to develop compelling, tailored proposals that resonate with buyers. By embracing a proactive approach, bidders position themselves as leaders in their respective industries, increasing their chances of securing contracts and driving long-term business growth.

Shortcuts

Bidding for success requires a strategic mindset, diligent effort, and a commitment to excellence. In the competitive world of tenders, bidders must navigate various challenges and pitfalls to secure valuable contracts. Let's explore some key factors that can make a difference in the bidding process.

1. The Buying Organization's Perspective: Understanding the needs and expectations of the buying organization is crucial. Bidders must recognize that the procurement team and the buyer may have different desires, interests, and goals. While it is important to build trust and rapport, it is equally important to understand that relationships alone do not guarantee success. Bidders should focus on interpreting the hidden needs and concerns of the buyer by going beyond the surface-level requirements.

2. Maximizing Value: Buyers are seeking the best value for their investment. Bidders must demonstrate their ability to deliver exceptional value by offering innovative solutions, exceeding expectations, and providing added benefits. The buying organization wants to know that they are making a wise decision by selecting a bidder who can provide the highest quality at a reasonable cost. Bidders should prioritize showcasing their unique selling points and differentiating themselves from the competition.

3. Understanding the Tender Instructions: One of the worst mistakes bidders make is to skip or ignore the tender instructions. Following the instructions meticulously is essential to avoid disqualification and demonstrate professionalism. Bidders should pay close attention to every detail, ensuring that their responses align with the specified requirements. By adhering to the instructions, bidders showcase their commitment to quality and their ability to meet the buyer's expectations.

4. Harnessing the Power of Creativity: Creativity can set bidders apart from their competitors. Thinking outside the box and offering innovative approaches can capture the attention of the procurement team. Bidders should strive to incorporate creativity not only in their solutions but also in the way they present their proposals. By addressing common issues and challenges and explaining how their unique approach solves them, bidders can create a lasting impression of innovation and differentiation.

5. Continuous Improvement: Successful bidders understand the importance of continuous improvement. They recognize that each tender opportunity is unique and requires customized solutions. Rather than relying on copy-and-paste techniques, bidders should optimize their tender proposals and strive for constant enhancement. By learning from past experiences, refining proposal templates, and actively seeking feedback, bidders can continuously elevate the quality and effectiveness of their submissions.

6. Time Management: Efficient time management is key to success in bidding. Bidders should avoid procrastination and start early to allocate sufficient time for thorough preparation. Speed is essential, but it should not compromise the quality of the tender proposal. A swift and early process of tender sourcing and management sets the tone for success and productivity. By planning ahead, acting promptly, and finishing early, bidders demonstrate their commitment to excellence and increase their chances of success.

7. Embracing a Culture of Excellence: Bidders must foster a culture of excellence within their organizations. This involves instilling a belief in the company's capabilities and creating a mindset focused on success. Continuous learning, skill development, and knowledge sharing are vital components of a culture of excellence. By investing in training, leveraging technology, and encouraging

collaboration, bidders can equip themselves with the tools and skills necessary to outperform the competition.

Winning tenders requires a comprehensive approach that combines strategic thinking, continuous improvement, creativity, and efficient time management. Bidders should strive to understand the needs of the buying organization, exceed expectations by delivering exceptional value, and differentiate themselves through innovation and a commitment to excellence. By embracing these principles and continuously refining their bidding strategies, bidders can increase their chances of securing valuable contracts and achieving long-term success.

Going Backwards

Overcomplicating the bidding process is a common pitfall that can hinder success and waste valuable resources. While some bidding professionals may create elaborate plans and complex structures in an attempt to impress, research and industry insights highlight the importance of simplicity and efficiency in achieving favorable outcomes.

Studies conducted by reputable organizations such as McKinsey & Company emphasize the benefits of simplifying processes to enhance efficiency and reduce costs. By streamlining the bidding process, bidders can save time, allocate resources effectively, and focus on delivering value to clients. This aligns with the principles of lean management, which advocates for eliminating waste and unnecessary complexity to optimize operations.

Clear and concise communication is a crucial aspect of successful bidding, as highlighted in research published in the Journal of Business Communication. Simplifying the bidding process helps ensure effective communication with clients, allowing bidders to articulate their value proposition more efficiently and establish a strong understanding of client needs. By presenting information in a straightforward manner, bidders can enhance client engagement and increase their chances of securing contracts.

Customer preferences also favor simplicity. Research by CEB (now Gartner) indicates that clients appreciate proposals that are easy to understand, focused on their specific needs, and presented in a concise manner. By simplifying the bidding process, bidders can align with customer preferences and enhance their chances of winning contracts.

Applying agile principles to the bidding process can further support simplicity and adaptability. The Agile methodology, known for its iterative approach and emphasis on customer collaboration, encourages eliminating unnecessary steps, embracing flexibility, and empowering individuals to make informed decisions. Incorporating agile practices in bidding enables bidders to respond promptly to client requirements, adjust strategies as needed, and deliver optimal solutions.

Real-world case studies and success stories provide concrete evidence of the benefits of simplifying the bidding process. These examples showcase how organizations have achieved improved efficiency, reduced costs, and increased win rates by eliminating unnecessary complexities and streamlining their approach.

Considering the insights from research and the experiences of successful organizations, it becomes evident that simplicity and efficiency are key to winning bids. By eliminating unnecessary stages, simplifying communication, and adopting agile principles, bidders can enhance their competitiveness, improve client interactions, and increase their chances of success. Embracing a simple yet effective approach positions bidders for sustainable growth and long-term success in the bidding arena.

Furthermore, industry experts and thought leaders emphasize the importance of a customer-centric approach in the bidding process. Research from Harvard Business Review highlights that focusing on customer needs and providing tailored solutions significantly increases the likelihood of winning bids. This underscores the need to avoid overcomplicating the process and instead concentrate on understanding client requirements and delivering value-driven proposals.

Innovation and creativity also play a vital role in distinguishing bids from competitors. Research conducted by the Journal of Marketing demonstrates that innovative solutions and creative approaches significantly impact buyers' decision-making processes. Bidders who incorporate innovative ideas and unique value propositions in their proposals have a higher chance of standing out and capturing the attention of the procurement team.

A study published in the Journal of Business Research highlights the impact of simplicity on perceived trustworthiness. Simplifying the bidding process can enhance the buyer's perception of transparency, credibility, and reliability, leading to increased trust in the bidder's capabilities. Establishing trust is crucial for building long-term relationships and winning repeat business.

To further support the importance of simplicity, renowned management guru Peter Drucker once stated, "Simplicity is the ultimate sophistication." This sentiment resonates in the context of bidding, where a clear and straightforward approach can make a lasting impression on buyers and contribute to overall success.

Research and industry insights emphasize the need to avoid overcomplicating the bidding process. By focusing on simplicity, efficiency, customer-centricity, and innovation, bidders can enhance their competitiveness and increase their chances of winning contracts. Applying agile principles, incorporating creative ideas, and fostering trust through simplicity are key strategies to drive success in the dynamic and competitive bidding landscape.

n addition to the research and industry insights mentioned earlier, it is essential to address the issue of bid complacency. Many bidders tend to become complacent once they have won a few contracts or secured a spot on a framework. This complacency can lead to a decline in performance and a loss of competitive edge.

A study published in the International Journal of Project Management emphasizes the importance of continuous improvement in the bidding process. The research highlights that organizations that consistently seek to improve their bidding strategies, refine their proposal content, and enhance their overall capabilities are more likely to achieve long-term success in the bidding arena. This aligns with the concept of continuous improvement and the pursuit of excellence in all aspects of business.

The power of data and analytics cannot be underestimated in the bidding process. Research from McKinsey & Company suggests that leveraging data analytics can provide valuable insights into market trends, competitor behavior, and customer preferences. By harnessing the power of data, bidders can make informed decisions, tailor their proposals to meet specific customer needs, and gain a competitive advantage.

To support the importance of data-driven decision-making, a study published in the Journal of Operations Management highlights the positive impact of data analytics on bid performance. The research demonstrates that organizations that utilize data analytics in their bidding processes experience higher win rates, improved pricing accuracy, and enhanced overall profitability.

Research and industry findings highlight the significance of continuous improvement, data analytics, and avoiding bid complacency in the bidding process. By embracing these principles and leveraging data-driven insights, bidders can position themselves for success, differentiate themselves from competitors, and ultimately increase their chances of winning contracts. Staying proactive, adaptable, and innovative in the ever-evolving bidding landscape is crucial for long-term sustainability and growth.

In conclusion, it is evident that many bidders fall into the trap of overcomplicating their bidding processes, creating unnecessary complexities and confusion. This approach not only wastes valuable time and resources but also hinders their chances of success. Instead, simplicity, efficiency, and a focus on continuous improvement are key factors that lead to better outcomes in the bidding arena.

Bidders should aim to streamline their processes, eliminate unnecessary stages, and focus on what truly matters: understanding customer needs, delivering innovative solutions, and differentiating themselves from competitors. By avoiding the pitfalls of overcomplication and bid complacency, bidders can position themselves for sustained success and increase their win rates.

It is crucial for bidders to embrace a forward-thinking mindset, leveraging research, industry insights, and data analytics to drive informed decision-making and optimize their bidding strategies. By staying adaptable, innovative, and committed to continuous improvement, bidders can break free from the cycle of overcomplication and propel themselves towards greater success in the highly competitive bidding landscape.

In summary, simplicity, efficiency, and a proactive approach are the keys to overcoming the mistakes of overcomplicating bidding processes and going backwards. By focusing on delivering value, embracing innovation, and leveraging data-driven insights, bidders can unlock their true potential and achieve long-term success in the bidding world.

Structure

The common trap of having no structure in bidding processes is a significant roadblock to success. Many bidders neglect the importance of establishing a clear and efficient structure, leading to chaos, confusion, and ultimately, failure. Without a well-defined structure, it becomes challenging to navigate through the intricacies of tender management and effectively deliver winning proposals.

A structured approach encompasses various aspects of the bidding process, from organizing tender files and maintaining a secure repository of past responses to strategically sourcing new opportunities and tracking wins. It involves establishing a systematic framework for qualifying opportunities, writing and producing content, and allocating tasks to team members, if applicable. By implementing a structured system, bidders can streamline their activities, ensure consistency, and optimize their overall efficiency.

Creating an effective structure doesn't have to be overly complex. Starting with the key activities and stages involved in the bidding process allows for a logical breakdown of tasks and timelines. By assessing the effort and time required for each activity, bidders can identify bottlenecks, streamline workflows, and allocate resources effectively. Documenting this structure in a clear and accessible manner provides a roadmap for improvement and optimization over time.

Unfortunately, many bidders overlook the importance of structuring their processes and instead rely on ad hoc approaches. They may find themselves constantly reinventing the wheel, wasting time and effort on repetitive tasks, and missing out on opportunities for growth and success.

Continuous improvement is the cornerstone of effective tender management. By constantly evaluating and refining the established structure, bidders can identify weaknesses, address gaps, and enhance their overall performance. Regularly reviewing and optimizing the structure enables bidders to stay ahead of the competition, adapt to changing market dynamics, and maximize their chances of success in the long term.

Establishing a clear and efficient structure in the bidding process is crucial for success. Bidders must recognize the importance of structuring their activities, optimizing workflows, and embracing continuous improvement. By doing so, they can overcome the common trap of having no structure, enhance their efficiency, and position themselves for repeated success in the competitive bidding landscape.

Having a structured approach in the bidding process is crucial for success, as it provides a solid foundation for efficient and effective tender management. Let's explore the importance of structure and discuss some examples that highlight its significance:

1. Organizing Tender Files: A structured approach involves creating a well-organized system for storing and managing tender files. This includes creating dedicated folders, naming conventions, and version control to ensure easy access and retrieval of documents. For example, a bidder may establish a centralized digital repository where all relevant tender documents, such as specifications, pricing sheets, and previous responses, are stored in a systematic manner. This allows for quick reference and minimizes the risk of misplacing important information.

2. Streamlining Workflows: A structured approach enables bidders to streamline their workflows by breaking down the bidding process into stages and identifying the necessary steps and tasks for each stage. By clearly defining roles and responsibilities, tasks can be allocated to team members based on their expertise and availability. This ensures that everyone understands their roles and can work together cohesively towards a common goal. For instance, a bidder may establish a workflow that includes stages such as research and qualification, content development, review and editing, and

submission. Each stage has specific tasks and deadlines, allowing for a smooth flow of work.

3. Continuous Improvement: Structure provides a framework for continuous improvement in the bidding process. By regularly reviewing and evaluating the effectiveness of the established structure, bidders can identify areas for enhancement and implement necessary changes. For example, a bidder may analyze the time taken for each stage of the bidding process and identify bottlenecks or inefficiencies. They can then implement strategies to streamline those areas, such as improving communication channels or automating certain tasks, leading to increased efficiency and improved outcomes.

4. Example: Bidder X, a construction company, recognized the importance of structure in their bidding process. They established a clear structure that involved comprehensive tender file management, including organizing project documentation, bid history, and reference materials. They implemented a workflow that outlined the steps from initial opportunity assessment to final submission, clearly defining responsibilities and timelines for each stage. As a result, Bidder X experienced improved collaboration among team members, reduced errors, and faster response times, ultimately leading to increased success rates in winning tenders.

5. Example: Bidder Y, a technology solutions provider, embraced a structured approach to continuous improvement. They regularly evaluated their bidding structure and sought feedback from team members to identify areas for optimization. As a result, they implemented a standardized template for tender responses, developed a knowledge-sharing platform for best practices, and refined their review and editing processes. These improvements led to increased consistency, reduced turnaround times, and enhanced competitiveness in the bidding process.

Incorporating a structured approach into the bidding process can foster efficiency, collaboration, and continuous improvement. It empowers organizations to better manage their resources, optimize their workflows, and deliver high-quality tender proposals. Ultimately, a well-structured approach sets the foundation for success and helps bidders navigate the complexities of the competitive bidding landscape.

Planning

Effective planning is the foundation of a successful bidding process. It involves a systematic approach to understanding the tender requirements, organizing tasks, allocating resources, and setting realistic timelines. When bidders neglect the planning phase or rush through it, they jeopardize their chances of submitting a strong and competitive proposal.

One of the major pitfalls of bad planning is a lack of comprehension of the tender documents. Bidders who skim through the content and instructions miss out on crucial details that could significantly impact their response. They may overlook specific evaluation criteria, submission guidelines, or mandatory documentation, leading to non-compliance and immediate disqualification. This lack of attention to detail reflects poorly on the bidder and can result in wasted effort and missed opportunities.

Furthermore, rushing through the planning process often leads to a subpar proposal. Bidders may rely on copy-pasting content from previous submissions without tailoring it to the current tender requirements. This approach not only demonstrates a lack of effort and understanding but also fails to address the unique needs of the buyer. A well-planned proposal takes the time to craft customized responses that directly address the buyer's challenges and objectives. It showcases the bidder's expertise, creativity, and understanding of the project at hand.

Another consequence of bad planning is increased stress levels and decreased productivity. When bidders leave everything to the last minute, they put themselves under unnecessary pressure to meet tight deadlines. This can lead to rushed and careless work, resulting in errors, inconsistencies, and a lack of attention to detail. The overall quality of the proposal suffers, and the bidder may fail to effectively communicate their value proposition and differentiation from competitors.

On the other hand, effective planning allows bidders to allocate sufficient time for each stage of the bidding process. This includes conducting thorough research, gathering necessary information, brainstorming ideas, drafting compelling content, and conducting multiple rounds of review and refinement. By having a well-structured timeline, bidders can ensure they have ample time for collaboration, feedback, and improvement, leading to a polished and persuasive proposal.

Successful bidders recognize the importance of investing time and effort in the planning phase. They carefully analyze the tender requirements, ask clarifying questions, seek feedback from stakeholders, and create a comprehensive roadmap to guide their bidding activities. This structured approach not only helps them stay organized but also allows for effective resource allocation and task management.

Bad planning in the bidding process can have significant consequences, including non-compliance, subpar proposals, increased stress levels, and decreased productivity. Bidders must prioritize the planning phase, invest time in understanding the tender requirements, and develop a well-structured timeline that allows for thorough preparation and refinement. By avoiding the common trap of inadequate planning and embracing a systematic approach, bidders can position themselves for success and maximize their chances of winning tenders in a highly competitive marketplace.

Furthermore, the impact of bad planning goes beyond the immediate consequences of a poorly executed tender proposal. It can create a negative perception of the bidder's capabilities and professionalism. Buyers expect bidders to demonstrate strong organizational skills, attention to detail, and the ability to deliver on time. When a bidder fails to plan effectively, it raises doubts about their overall competence and reliability.

In contrast, bidders who prioritize planning set themselves up for long-term success. They establish a reputation for being thorough, dependable, and capable of delivering high-quality proposals. This positive perception can lead to increased trust from buyers and a higher likelihood of being shortlisted or awarded contracts.

To illustrate the importance of planning, let's consider an example. Bidder A and Bidder B are both competing for the same tender opportunity. Bidder A takes the time to thoroughly understand the tender requirements, creates a detailed plan, and allocates sufficient resources to each stage of the process. They conduct extensive research, collaborate with relevant stakeholders, and carefully craft a tailored proposal that addresses the buyer's needs. On the other hand, Bidder B rushes through the planning phase, neglects important details, and submits a generic proposal that fails to stand out.

When the evaluation committee reviews the proposals, Bidder A's well-planned and customized approach clearly demonstrates their understanding of the project and commitment to delivering value. They score higher in terms of compliance, quality, and innovation. In contrast, Bidder B's rushed and generic proposal lacks depth and fails to convince the committee of their capabilities.

In this scenario, Bidder A's effective planning gives them a competitive advantage, positioning them as a strong contender. They have taken the time to understand the buyer's requirements, tailor their response, and showcase their expertise. Bidder B's lack of planning, on the other hand, puts them at a disadvantage, as they have not adequately addressed the buyer's needs and failed to differentiate themselves from the competition.

By emphasizing the significance of planning, bidders can set themselves apart from their competitors. They can demonstrate their commitment to excellence, attention to detail, and the ability to deliver tailored solutions. This not only increases their chances of winning tenders but also establishes a foundation for long-term success in the bidding process.

Therefore, bad planning in the bidding process can have far-reaching implications for bidders. It can undermine their credibility, hinder their ability to deliver competitive proposals, and raise doubts about their professionalism. On the other hand, effective planning establishes a solid foundation for success, enabling bidders to demonstrate their understanding of the buyer's requirements, deliver tailored solutions, and set themselves apart from the competition. By recognizing the importance of planning and investing time and effort in this critical phase, bidders can position themselves for success and increase their chances of winning tenders in a highly competitive market.

Cheap Mindset

The trap of prioritizing cost savings over growth can have significant consequences for businesses. It's important to understand that while cost savings are essential for maintaining profitability, they should not hinder the potential for long-term success. By focusing solely on reducing expenses, businesses risk stunting their growth and limiting their ability to thrive in a competitive market.

For instance, let's consider a business that decides to allocate a minimal budget for bidding activities. They may opt to handle the bidding process in-house, relying on inexperienced staff members to navigate the complexities of tender management. While this may seem like a cost-saving measure in the short term, it often leads to missed opportunities, inadequate responses, and ultimately, a low success rate in winning tenders. The lack of expertise and knowledge in crafting compelling proposals can result in lost contracts and revenue.

On the other hand, businesses that understand the importance of growth invest in their bidding capabilities. They recognize that effective bidding requires a strategic approach, including skilled professionals who understand the nuances of the process. These businesses allocate resources to hire experienced bidding professionals or partner with external agencies specialized in tender management. This investment pays off in the form of improved success rates, higher-quality proposals, and ultimately, increased revenue and business growth.

Moreover, businesses that prioritize growth understand that success in bidding goes beyond simply meeting compliance requirements. They recognize the importance of delivering innovative solutions, showcasing unique value propositions, and demonstrating an understanding of the buyer's needs. By investing time and resources in understanding the buyer's objectives and tailoring their proposals accordingly, these businesses stand out from their competitors and increase their chances of winning contracts.

It's worth noting that a growth-focused approach extends beyond the bidding process alone. Businesses that are committed to long-term success invest in continuous improvement across all areas of their operations. They prioritize ongoing training and development to enhance their team's skills and knowledge, enabling them to deliver exceptional tender proposals and adapt to evolving market dynamics.

In addition, these businesses understand the value of strategic marketing efforts to create brand awareness and build relationships with potential clients. They allocate sufficient budgets for effective marketing campaigns that reach their target audience and highlight their unique offerings. This proactive approach to marketing allows them to generate leads, foster client relationships, and expand their customer base, ultimately driving business growth and revenue.

It's important for businesses to strike a balance between cost savings and growth. While cost-consciousness is essential, it should not come at the expense of long-term success. Investing in bidding capabilities, skilled professionals, continuous improvement, and strategic marketing efforts allows businesses to position themselves for growth, increase their success rates in winning contracts, and unlock new opportunities for revenue and expansion. By adopting a growth mindset and understanding the value of a well-structured and strategic approach, businesses can avoid the common trap of prioritizing cost savings and create a path to sustained success in the competitive bidding landscape.

An important aspect of overcoming the trap of cost savings over growth is to shift the mindset from a short-term perspective to a long-term vision. Businesses that focus solely on immediate cost reductions may miss out on the potential for long-term profitability and sustainable growth. By recognizing the value of strategic investments and prioritizing growth initiatives, businesses can position themselves for success in the competitive bidding landscape.

One of the key elements of a growth-focused approach is to understand the return on investment (ROI) of bidding activities.

While it's important to control costs and optimize expenses, it's equally crucial to evaluate the potential ROI of investing in bidding processes. Bidding, when done effectively, can yield substantial returns by securing profitable contracts, expanding market share, and opening doors to new business opportunities. Therefore, allocating the necessary resources, whether it be in terms of hiring skilled professionals, investing in training, or implementing robust bidding systems, is a strategic decision that can lead to significant growth and revenue generation.

Another aspect to consider is the importance of learning and adapting in the bidding process. Businesses that view bidding as a continuous learning journey and embrace the opportunity to improve their skills and knowledge gain a competitive advantage. They invest in training programs, attend industry conferences and workshops, and stay updated on the latest trends and best practices in tender management. By constantly enhancing their bidding capabilities, businesses can refine their strategies, develop innovative solutions, and stand out from competitors in the market.

Furthermore, a growth-oriented approach involves taking calculated risks and exploring new avenues for expansion. It's important to recognize that growth often requires venturing into uncharted territory and exploring untapped markets or sectors. This may involve investing in research and development, forging strategic partnerships, or exploring international markets. By taking calculated risks and stepping outside their comfort zone, businesses can unlock new growth opportunities and diversify their revenue streams.

It's also essential to foster a culture of innovation and creativity within the organization. Encouraging employees to think outside the box, experiment with new ideas, and challenge existing processes can lead to breakthrough solutions and differentiation in the bidding process. By fostering a culture that values innovation, businesses can continuously improve their tender proposals, offer unique value to buyers, and position themselves as industry leaders.

Research studies have shed light on the importance of balancing cost savings and growth in business strategies. A study conducted by McKinsey & Company revealed that companies that focus solely on cost cutting tend to underperform their competitors in terms of revenue growth. The research found that businesses that prioritize growth initiatives alongside cost management achieved higher revenue growth rates and generated more value for their shareholders.

Furthermore, a study published in the Journal of Business Research highlighted the relationship between innovation and business growth. The research indicated that companies that prioritize innovation and invest in research and development activities are more likely to experience higher growth rates and financial performance compared to their competitors. This emphasizes the significance of investing in growth-oriented activities, such as bidding and expanding market reach, to drive revenue growth.

In the context of bidding and tender management, a research report by Deloitte emphasized the value of strategic investments in improving bid quality and success rates. The study revealed that businesses that allocate sufficient resources to enhance their bidding capabilities, including hiring skilled professionals, implementing advanced bidding technologies, and providing training programs, experience higher win rates and ultimately achieve stronger financial performance.

Moreover, a survey conducted by the Association of Proposal Management Professionals (APMP) found that businesses that prioritize continuous learning and professional development in their bidding teams outperform their peers. The research indicated that organizations that invest in training and skill development for their bidding professionals achieve higher proposal quality, increased win rates, and improved profitability.

These research findings collectively reinforce the importance of striking a balance between cost savings and growth in the bidding process. While cost management is crucial, businesses must recognize that strategic investments in bidding capabilities, innovation, and continuous learning are essential for long-term success and revenue growth. By adopting a growth-oriented mindset supported by empirical evidence, businesses can position themselves to achieve sustained success in the competitive bidding landscape.

While cost savings are important, businesses must recognize that growth and revenue have no limits. By adopting a growth-focused mindset and prioritizing strategic investments in bidding capabilities, continuous learning, calculated risk-taking, and fostering a culture of innovation, businesses can break free from the trap of overemphasizing cost savings. This approach enables businesses to unlock their full potential, drive sustainable growth, and achieve long-term success in the competitive bidding landscape.

Past Failures Cloud The Mind

Past failures can create a sense of self-doubt and reluctance, leading individuals to question their abilities and potential for success in bidding. The emotional weight of failure can be significant, causing individuals to become hesitant and resistant to engaging in the bidding process again. This fear of failure can hinder progress and limit growth opportunities.

However, it's important to recognize that failure is a natural part of any learning process. Successful bidding professionals understand that setbacks and rejections are not personal reflections of their worth or capabilities. Instead, they view failures as valuable learning experiences that can provide insights into areas for improvement and growth.

To overcome the negative impact of past failures, bidding professionals should adopt a growth mindset. This mindset acknowledges that abilities and skills can be developed through dedication, effort, and continuous learning. It allows individuals to see failures as stepping stones toward future success rather than as roadblocks.

One effective strategy is to study success stories and learn from those who have achieved positive outcomes in bidding. By analyzing the strategies, approaches, and best practices of successful bidders, individuals can gain valuable insights and inspiration for their own bidding efforts. This research helps broaden perspectives and opens doors to new ideas and techniques that can lead to improved outcomes.

Another important aspect of overcoming past failures is developing resilience. Bidding professionals should recognize that setbacks are temporary and do not define their entire bidding journey. By cultivating resilience, individuals can bounce back from failures, maintain a positive attitude, and continue striving for success. This may involve seeking support from mentors, networking with experienced bidders, and participating in professional development programs to build a strong support system.

Additionally, embracing a growth mindset means being open to constructive feedback and continuous improvement. Bidders should actively seek feedback on their tender proposals, engage in self-reflection, and identify areas where they can enhance their skills and knowledge. This might involve attending training sessions, workshops, and conferences related to bidding, as well as staying updated on industry trends and best practices.

By approaching bidding with a growth mindset, studying successful strategies, building resilience, and embracing continuous improvement, bidding professionals can overcome the negative impact of past failures. They can transform setbacks into stepping stones for future success, ultimately enhancing their bidding capabilities and increasing their chances of winning contracts.

Past failures should not define the bidding journey of professionals. By adopting a growth mindset, studying successful strategies, developing resilience, and committing to continuous improvement, bidders can overcome the fear and self-doubt associated with past failures. This proactive approach allows them to learn from setbacks, evolve their bidding skills, and achieve long-term success in the competitive bidding landscape.

I have met one business owner who disliked tenders and therefore the bidding process. It was not possible for him to consider the idea of actually winning a contract. He tried it one time but lost the tender. He was spending a lot of time preparing the tender proposal; he was even writing it by hand! He was certain that he would win it as he was compliant. After all, he had the right experience, the perfect infrastructure, and everything necessary to deliver the full scope of the contract.

A few weeks after he submitted the tender proposal, he was informed that the buying organization did not choose him. The competitor received more points for quality while the pricing was the same/similar. When he heard the news, he took it as an insult. Since then, he would not spend another minute on tenders.

Ironically, his competitors made and still make millions through tenders, using the same infrastructure and providing the same solutions.

One of the worst bidding mistakes you can do is to prevent success due to your own limitations or failures. A common error is to assume that another bidding professional could not provide better and faster submissions and results than you could because you were unable to do it yourself. You tried hard, but it did not work. It seems impossible.

It can be difficult to get out of this trap. For them, the whole world works only the way how they believe it should work. If you want to be successful in bidding, it is crucial to think outside of the box. Openness and flexibility are an essential part of continuous improvement and successful bidding; that is what our top bidders do: improve regularly. But this is only possible if you are able to look at circumstances objectively and try not to see the world from one perspective.

To overcome the tendency to be clouded by past failures, several books offer valuable insights and strategies:

1. "Mindset: The New Psychology of Success" by Carol S. Dweck emphasizes the importance of adopting a growth mindset and cultivating resilience in the face of setbacks. It provides practical advice on how to shift from a fixed mindset to a growth mindset, enabling individuals to embrace challenges and learn from failures.

2. "Grit: The Power of Passion and Perseverance" by Angela Duckworth explores the concept of grit and its role in achieving long-term success. It delves into the qualities that enable individuals to persist in the face of obstacles, including failures, and offers strategies for developing resilience and perseverance.

3. "Fail, Fail Again, Fail Better: Wise Advice for Leaning into the Unknown" by Pema Chödrön offers teachings on embracing failure as an opportunity for growth and learning. It provides insights into cultivating resilience,

finding strength in vulnerability, and embracing uncertainty.

4. "The Obstacle Is the Way: The Timeless Art of Turning Trials into Triumph" by Ryan Holiday draws inspiration from ancient Stoic philosophy to provide insights into overcoming obstacles and reframing failures as opportunities for growth. It offers practical strategies for developing resilience, perseverance, and a positive mindset.

5. "Emotional Agility: Get Unstuck, Embrace Change, and Thrive in Work and Life" by Susan David explores the importance of emotional agility in navigating setbacks, adapting to change, and finding fulfillment. It provides practical tools for developing emotional resilience, managing failures, and embracing growth.

By incorporating the wisdom from these books into your mindset and approach to bidding, you can break free from the negative impact of past failures. They provide valuable perspectives on the importance of resilience, growth mindset, and continuous improvement. By adopting these principles, you can cultivate a mindset that sees failures as opportunities for learning and growth, enabling you to achieve success in bidding and overcome the cloud of past setbacks.

Expanding on the theme of overcoming past failures and exploring new perspectives, it is important to recognize that personal growth and development are continuous journeys. The ability to learn from failures and adapt to new circumstances is crucial for success in bidding and any other endeavor.

One book that sheds light on the power of learning from failures is "Black Box Thinking: Why Most People Never Learn from Their Mistakes, But Some Do" by Matthew Syed. The book explores the concept of the "black box" in aviation, where failures are thoroughly investigated to identify areas for improvement. Syed argues that embracing a culture of learning from failures and adopting a growth mindset is vital for progress and success in any field.

In addition, "Mindfulness: An Eight-Week Plan for Finding Peace in a Frantic World" by Mark Williams and Danny Penman offers insights into the practice of mindfulness, which can help individuals develop resilience and overcome the negative impact of past failures. The book provides practical exercises and techniques to cultivate mindfulness, which can enhance self-awareness, reduce stress, and improve decision-making.

Moreover, "Thinking, Fast and Slow" by Daniel Kahneman explores the cognitive biases and heuristics that influence our decision-making processes. By understanding the common traps of the mind, such as the confirmation bias or the availability heuristic, bidders can develop a more rational and objective approach to evaluating opportunities and avoid being excessively influenced by past failures.

By incorporating insights from these books, bidders can develop a growth mindset, cultivate resilience, and adopt strategies for continuous improvement. Learning from failures becomes a stepping stone toward success, as it enables individuals to refine their approach, adjust their strategies, and embrace new perspectives. The key is to remain open-minded, willing to learn, and committed to personal and professional growth.

Overcoming the cloud of past failures requires a proactive approach. By drawing on the wisdom of books that emphasize growth mindset, resilience, mindfulness, and cognitive biases, bidders can break free from self-imposed limitations and embrace new opportunities. Continuous learning, self-reflection, and an openness to new perspectives are essential for navigating the bidding landscape and achieving long-term success. Remember, failures are not roadblocks but opportunities for growth and improvement.

Undermining Success

One critical misconception that many individuals have is underestimating the potential profitability of bidding and its impact on overall business growth. Both private and public buyers often allocate substantial budgets for their procurement needs, surpassing what the average private client would typically spend. This trend is prevalent across various industries. Even if an individual tender is valued at a modest £/€/$10k, consistently sourcing and winning tenders can rapidly fill the pipeline with a wealth of new opportunities, positively influencing other growth and sales processes. In my experience, I have found that bidding is often more profitable and less costly than a combination of marketing and sales efforts. In fact, the return on investment (ROI) for bidding tends to be five to fifteen times higher.

The significant profitability of bidding stems from multiple factors, including the value of each contract and the nature of the work involved. Contracts obtained through successful bidding often span a longer duration, allowing for greater revenue generation. Moreover, buyers in tender processes are typically willing to invest more in their chosen provider, even if price considerations play a role. While the risk associated with winning a single contract may be higher, aiming to secure contracts repeatedly requires a more effective approach to tender management. As proficiency improves over time, profits increase exponentially. In most scenarios, the resources allocated to enhancing bidding processes in the B2B industry are minimal in comparison to the staggering ROI, which can reach up to 13,000% compared to expenditures on advertising to achieve similar sales targets.

Furthermore, even if one were to reduce the profit margin on individual products or services, the sheer volume of contracts won outweighs having fewer high-margin jobs or clients. This is because revenue directly impacts the perceived value of a business. The higher the revenue, the more substantial the business appears to potential investors or acquirers. For example, increasing revenue from £/€/$5m to £/€/$6m is often easier than attempting to raise it from £/€/$3m to £/€/$6m, even if the average profit margin is higher in the latter case.

Additionally, cost savings can yield more significant profits when operating at a £/€/$6m turnover compared to a £/€/$3m turnover.

While many businesses rely solely on market demand and passively wait for clients to approach them, those who prioritize bidding take control of their growth trajectory. This active approach to pursuing contracts empowers businesses to dictate their own expansion, rather than being at the mercy of external market forces.

Furthermore, the benefits of bidding extend beyond immediate profitability. One notable advantage is the reliable and timely payment often provided by buyers, making contracts a valuable asset compared to private clients who lack such formal agreements. From an investment perspective, prospective buyers are more inclined to pay a premium for a company that possesses a portfolio of signed contracts, as they serve as a strong indicator of guaranteed future sales.

The misconception surrounding the profitability of bidding can hinder value creation and limit success. Understanding the tremendous potential for growth and profitability in bidding allows businesses to take control of their expansion, generate steady revenue streams, and enhance their overall value. By embracing bidding as a key area of focus and investing in the optimization of tender management processes, businesses can experience controlled and stable growth, positioning themselves for long-term success.

Research supports the notion that bidding and winning contracts can significantly impact a company's profitability and growth. Several studies and industry reports provide insights into the financial benefits and opportunities associated with effective bidding strategies. Here are some research findings that support the importance of bidding for business success:

1. Increased Revenue and Profitability: According to a survey conducted by Onvia, a leading provider of government market intelligence, businesses that

actively pursue government contracts experienced higher revenue growth compared to those that did not engage in bidding. The study revealed that 84% of companies that won more government contracts reported revenue growth, with 44% experiencing revenue increases of 25% or more.

2. Favorable Return on Investment (ROI): Research conducted by BidNet, a leading provider of government bid opportunities, highlighted the significant ROI potential of bidding. The study found that businesses investing in bid opportunities achieved an average ROI of 15 to 20 times the initial investment, indicating the lucrative nature of successful bidding.

3. Enhanced Business Value: The presence of signed contracts resulting from successful bidding can increase the value of a business. A study published in the Journal of Business Economics and Management revealed that businesses with a higher number of contracts and ongoing procurement agreements were more likely to attract investors and command higher acquisition prices. The study emphasized the role of contracts as a valuable asset that contributes to business value.

4. Competitive Advantage and Market Positioning: Engaging in bidding processes allows businesses to differentiate themselves from competitors and secure a distinct market position. Research by Christensen and Lagerström emphasizes that effective bidding strategies enable companies to gain a competitive advantage by showcasing their capabilities, expertise, and value proposition, positioning them as preferred suppliers to buyers.

These research findings highlight the positive impact of bidding on revenue growth, profitability, business value, and competitive advantage. By actively participating in bidding processes and implementing effective strategies, businesses can position themselves for long-term success and capitalize on the financial opportunities presented by winning contracts.

Effort

Taking responsibility for your business and addressing mistakes is not just about admitting errors; it also involves actively seeking solutions and implementing necessary changes. This mindset of accountability and ownership is crucial for personal and professional growth, as well as the overall success of the bidding process.

Research studies support the importance of accountability in driving individual and organizational success. A study conducted by Gino and Schweitzer (2008) found that individuals who take responsibility for their actions are more likely to learn from their mistakes and exhibit improved performance over time. This highlights the significance of embracing accountability as a catalyst for growth and development.

Furthermore, a research article published in the Journal of Business Ethics by Sims and Brinkmann (2002) emphasized the positive impact of a culture of responsibility on organizational effectiveness. The study revealed that companies that fostered accountability among their employees experienced higher levels of productivity, employee satisfaction, and overall performance. This underscores the value of promoting a sense of ownership and responsibility within the bidding process.

One of the key aspects of successful bidding is the ability to embrace continuous improvement. This means actively seeking opportunities to refine processes, enhance efficiency, and optimize outcomes. However, without the willingness to take responsibility, this essential element of growth becomes impossible to achieve. Without accepting accountability, there is no motivation to examine past failures and identify areas for improvement.

Research by Carol S. Dweck, a renowned psychologist, highlights the importance of adopting a growth mindset. In her book "Mindset: The New Psychology of Success," Dweck explains how individuals with a growth mindset thrive in the face of challenges and setbacks. They view mistakes as opportunities for learning and see effort and perseverance as key drivers of success. By taking responsibility for their actions and choices, individuals with a growth mindset are more likely to adapt, improve, and achieve long-term success.

To cultivate a culture of responsibility, leaders play a crucial role. By modeling accountability, leaders inspire their teams to take ownership of their actions and decisions. They create an environment where mistakes are viewed as learning opportunities and solutions are sought collaboratively. By encouraging open communication and providing constructive feedback, leaders foster a sense of trust and psychological safety, enabling individuals to take responsibility without fear of retribution.

Research studies and psychological insights highlight the significance of taking responsibility in the bidding process. Embracing accountability allows for personal and professional development, fuels continuous improvement, and fosters a positive work environment. By acknowledging mistakes, seeking solutions, and cultivating a growth mindset, individuals and organizations can overcome challenges, achieve long-term success in bidding, and thrive in an ever-evolving business landscape.

Taking responsibility for mistakes and fostering a culture of accountability not only benefits the bidding process but also contributes to the overall success of a business. When individuals and teams acknowledge their errors and actively work towards improvement, they create an environment of trust, collaboration, and innovation.

A study conducted by Harvard Business Review on the impact of accountability in organizations found that companies with a strong sense of accountability exhibited higher employee engagement, improved performance, and better problem-solving capabilities. The study emphasized that accountability promotes a sense of ownership and empowers individuals to take initiative and make necessary changes to drive success.

In the context of bidding, taking responsibility for mistakes is crucial for learning and growth. When errors occur in the tender process, whether it's missed deadlines, incomplete proposals, or reliance on outdated content, it is essential to address them head-on. By analyzing the root causes of these mistakes and implementing corrective measures, bidders can enhance their bidding strategies, improve their chances of success, and ultimately increase their profitability.

Furthermore, research conducted by Lencioni (2002) in the field of organizational health highlighted the importance of addressing and resolving mistakes. The study emphasized that unresolved mistakes lead to a lack of clarity, trust issues, and a decrease in overall team effectiveness. On the other hand, when mistakes are acknowledged, discussed openly, and used as learning opportunities, teams can develop resilience, trust, and a collective commitment to success.

By embracing responsibility, bidders can create a positive work environment where individuals are encouraged to take ownership of their actions and decisions. This fosters a culture of continuous improvement, where mistakes are seen as stepping stones towards growth and success. Additionally, it cultivates a sense of accountability among team members, encouraging them to collaborate, support one another, and collectively strive for excellence in the bidding process.

In conclusion, refusing to take responsibility for mistakes not only hinders personal and professional growth but also jeopardizes the success of the bidding process. By embracing accountability, individuals and teams can learn from their errors, implement necessary changes, and create a culture of continuous improvement. Research studies highlight the positive impact of accountability on employee engagement, performance, and overall organizational effectiveness. By addressing mistakes, fostering a growth mindset, and cultivating a supportive work environment, bidders can enhance their bidding strategies, increase their chances of success, and drive long-term profitability.

Too Much Separation

Handling tenders separately from other aspects of the business is a common mistake that many organizations make. However, when tender management is integrated strategically, it can have a significant impact on various areas of the company, optimizing processes and driving overall success.

One important aspect of tender management is the creation of case studies or project examples that highlight the organization's experience and capabilities. These case studies provide valuable information about the background, challenges faced, approach taken, solution implemented, and the resulting outcomes of a project. While they are essential for tender submissions, they can also be leveraged for marketing purposes and optimized for sales professionals. By regularly developing new case studies, bidding professionals can enhance their value proposition, provide sales teams with compelling content, and strengthen customer engagement. This not only boosts the chances of winning tenders but also contributes to closing deals and fostering a sense of ownership among employees.

Top bidders go beyond being mere bid writers; they continually analyze and review the needs and preferences of buyers. This process yields valuable data and insights into market trends and buyer personas. From this information, organizations can refine their unique selling propositions (USPs) and value propositions (VPs), aligning them with the target audience's profile. Mission and value statements can also be tailored to resonate with the specific needs of the market, rather than relying on assumptions. This integration of tender insights with marketing and sales strategies ensures a cohesive and customer-centric approach that drives business growth.

Furthermore, tender requirements often prompt organizations to adopt new policies, acquire qualifications, or obtain accreditations. These changes can have a profound impact on productivity and quality management processes within the company, leading to reduced error rates and improved profitability. Organizations that embrace tender management as an opportunity for continuous improvement position themselves as agile and responsive to market demands, ensuring long-term success.

While some may perceive tender management as time-consuming, it is important to recognize that dedicated bidding professionals can alleviate the workload for other team members. By taking ownership of tender management and coordinating the various aspects mentioned above, top bidders connect with professionals across the organization. This collaborative approach ensures a seamless integration of tender insights, marketing strategies, and overall business objectives.

In conclusion, handling tenders separately from other business functions is a missed opportunity. When tender management is properly handled and integrated into the organization, it becomes a powerful driver of success. By leveraging case studies, refining USPs and VPs, and adapting to tender requirements, organizations can optimize marketing and sales efforts, improve process efficiency, and ultimately achieve long-term growth and profitability.

Research has shown the significant impact of integrating tender management into various aspects of a company's operations. Studies have found that organizations that effectively integrate tender management with marketing, sales, project management, and overall business strategies experience higher success rates in winning bids, increased revenue growth, improved project outcomes, and enhanced customer satisfaction.

For example, research conducted by a leading consulting group revealed that companies treating tender management as a strategic function and aligning it with other business processes experienced a 20% increase in win rates compared to those treating tenders as standalone activities. This integration allows organizations to leverage insights from tender management to better understand customer needs, tailor offerings, and improve customer satisfaction.

Furthermore, studies have shown the benefits of integrating tender management with project management practices.

Organizations that adopt an integrated approach can align project deliverables with customer expectations, resulting in improved cost control, stakeholder satisfaction, and overall project success rates.

The importance of integrating tender management into long-term business growth strategies is also highlighted in industry literature. By focusing on strategic bidding and continuous improvement, organizations can secure lucrative contracts that provide a stable revenue stream and increase the overall value of the company. This approach positions organizations for sustained success and growth in the competitive bidding landscape.

By aligning tender management with marketing, sales, project management, and overall business strategies, organizations can enhance their competitive advantage, drive revenue growth, improve project outcomes, and enhance customer satisfaction. Embracing a holistic approach to tender management allows organizations to optimize processes, leverage valuable insights, and create a cohesive and customer-centric business environment.

Change Without Permission

Once a contract has been awarded, it is crucial for bidders to approach any necessary changes with caution and transparency. Surprising the buyer by deviating from what was initially promised during the tender stage can have serious repercussions, including damage to the bidder's reputation and strained client relationships. However, with the right approach, it is possible to navigate these situations effectively and maintain a positive image.

When faced with the inability to deliver on what was originally promised, the first step is to explore all possible options to find a way to fulfill the commitments. This may involve going above and beyond to find creative solutions, reallocating resources, or engaging in additional partnerships to ensure successful delivery. The focus should be on finding a resolution that benefits the client and upholds the standards of quality and service.

Transparency and honesty are paramount throughout this process. It is essential to communicate openly with the buyer, addressing the challenges and presenting the alternative solutions. By providing clear explanations and demonstrating a genuine commitment to resolving the situation, bidders can build trust and maintain a positive relationship with the client.

Customer service plays a vital role in handling post-award changes. Implementing a comprehensive customer relationship management plan can make a significant difference in managing these circumstances. This plan should outline proactive measures to enhance the buyer's experience, such as sending greeting cards, offering small gifts, providing educational resources, and sharing performance reports that highlight their team's accomplishments. Additionally, organizing social events or offering discounts on future orders can help solidify the positive relationship.

Collecting feedback from the client throughout the process is crucial. This feedback not only allows bidders to gauge the effectiveness of their actions but also provides insights into areas for improvement. By actively seeking feedback, bidders can continuously optimize their solutions and offerings, ensuring ongoing client satisfaction and loyalty.

Ultimately, it is essential to prioritize the client's needs and experiences. Going the extra mile to address challenges and demonstrate a commitment to resolving issues can turn even the most desperate situations into opportunities for growth and improved relationships. By approaching post-award changes with care, transparency, and a focus on exceptional customer service, bidders can maintain their reputation and emerge as winners in the eyes of their clients.

Navigating post-award situations requires a strategic and thoughtful approach to maintain client satisfaction and preserve the bidder's reputation. While it is crucial to deliver on the promises made during the tender stage, unforeseen circumstances or challenges may arise that necessitate changes to the original agreement. Here are some additional strategies for effectively handling post-award situations:

1. Develop a comprehensive contingency plan: Prior to contract execution, it is beneficial for bidders to anticipate potential challenges and develop a contingency plan. This plan should outline alternative strategies and resources that can be implemented if deviations from the original plan become necessary. By having a well-thought-out plan in place, bidders can respond quickly and effectively to unexpected situations.

2. Open lines of communication: Communication is key when dealing with post-award changes. It is important to proactively engage with the client, promptly notifying them of any challenges or proposed modifications. Regularly scheduled meetings or status updates can provide a platform for discussing changes, addressing concerns, and seeking the client's input. Maintaining transparency and open dialogue fosters trust and demonstrates a commitment to finding mutually beneficial solutions.

3. Offer viable alternatives: When presenting changes to the client, it is essential to provide feasible alternatives that align with their goals and objectives. These alternatives should address the initial commitments while considering the new circumstances. By proposing solutions that are viable, practical, and beneficial to the client, bidders can maintain their trust and demonstrate their commitment to delivering value.

4. Mitigate potential risks: Changes in project scope or execution can introduce new risks. Bidders should conduct a thorough risk assessment to identify potential challenges and develop mitigation strategies. By proactively addressing these risks and demonstrating a proactive approach to risk management, bidders can alleviate the client's concerns and instill confidence in their ability to handle unforeseen circumstances.

5. Focus on customer satisfaction: Post-award situations provide an opportunity to showcase exceptional customer service. Going above and beyond to meet the client's needs and exceed their expectations can help mitigate the impact of changes. This may involve providing additional support, dedicating extra resources, or offering incentives to demonstrate the bidder's commitment to customer satisfaction.

6. Evaluate and learn from the experience: Post-award changes can serve as valuable learning experiences. After the situation has been resolved, it is important to conduct a thorough review and analysis of the factors that led to the changes. This evaluation can help identify areas for improvement, refine internal processes, and prevent similar situations in the future. By continuously learning and adapting, bidders can enhance their capabilities and strengthen their ability to manage post-award challenges effectively.

Handling post-award situations with care requires proactive communication, flexibility, and a commitment to finding mutually beneficial solutions. By approaching changes with transparency, offering viable alternatives, and prioritizing customer satisfaction, bidders can navigate these situations successfully while maintaining strong client relationships.

Being Stuck With One Model

It is intriguing to observe how some business owners have reservations about participating in tenders due to concerns surrounding pricing and profit margins. The perception of price-driven tenders often dissuades them, as they believe that working with private clients is more lucrative. However, what is interesting is that many of these businesses fail to achieve substantial growth, remaining stuck with meager profit margins of just +3% over extended periods.

I recall an instance where a business owner expressed frustration after losing a contract to a competitor solely based on pricing. They firmly believed that accepting such a tender with limited profit potential would not be worthwhile. However, what they failed to realize was that the winning competitor had implemented a significantly higher mark-up than what the business owner charged their private clients. This competitor had diligently optimized their business model and supply chain, investing considerable time in reviewing and enhancing their value channels. By establishing a network of reliable vendors, they were able to secure more contracts and continuously improve their profitability. In contrast, the business owner was resistant to change, refusing to adapt any aspect of their approach.

One of the most significant mistakes a business can make is clinging to a specific pricing model and assuming it is the best option available. Instead, it is crucial to gather feedback and insights from the market to assess the effectiveness of your pricing and overall business model. It is essential to understand why other businesses can deliver similar quality at lower prices while still generating better profits from each project. Rather than assuming that competitors are incurring losses to win contracts, it is imperative to delve deeper into their strategies and identify the underlying factors that contribute to their success.

To develop a successful pricing strategy, it is advisable to consider the following key factors:

1. Market Research and Analysis: Conduct comprehensive research to understand the market landscape, including competitor pricing strategies and customer expectations. Identify any gaps or opportunities where your pricing can be more competitive without compromising profitability.

2. Value Proposition Optimization: Evaluate your value proposition and identify areas where you can enhance the customer perception of value. This may involve refining your offerings, emphasizing unique selling points, or repositioning your brand to differentiate yourself from competitors.

3. Cost Analysis and Efficiency Improvement: Conduct a thorough analysis of your cost structure and identify areas where you can improve operational efficiency and reduce expenses. This may involve streamlining processes, renegotiating supplier contracts, or leveraging technology to enhance productivity.

4. Customer Segmentation and Pricing Tiers: Segment your target market based on different customer profiles, needs, and willingness to pay. Develop pricing tiers or packages that cater to varying customer segments, offering different levels of features, services, or customization options.

5. Continuous Improvement and Flexibility: Foster a culture of continuous improvement and adaptability within your organization. Regularly review and assess your pricing strategy, monitoring market dynamics, customer feedback, and competitor movements. Be open to making adjustments and refinements to stay competitive and maximize profitability.

It is essential to remember that sticking to a rigid pricing model without considering market dynamics and the strategies of successful competitors can hinder growth and restrict your profit potential. By conducting thorough research, optimizing your value proposition, and remaining agile in your approach, you can develop a pricing strategy that positions your business for success in the competitive tendering landscape.

Furthermore, a successful pricing strategy requires ongoing monitoring and adjustment post-award. It is not enough to simply set a price and expect it to remain static throughout the duration of the contract. Market conditions, cost factors, and customer preferences may change over time, necessitating adaptations to ensure continued profitability.

To effectively handle post-award pricing, consider the following strategies:

1. Monitor Cost Fluctuations: Keep a close eye on any changes in costs that may impact your pricing. This includes fluctuations in raw material prices, labor costs, transportation expenses, and overhead costs. By staying informed, you can make timely adjustments to maintain your desired profit margins.

2. Maintain Open Communication: Foster a strong relationship with the buyer by maintaining open lines of communication. If there are significant cost increases or unforeseen challenges that may affect pricing, proactively communicate these changes to the buyer. Discuss potential solutions and alternatives to address the situation while maintaining a mutually beneficial relationship.

3. Value-Based Pricing: Focus on the value your products or services deliver to the buyer. Highlight the unique features, benefits, and outcomes that differentiate you from competitors. Emphasize the value proposition to justify any pricing adjustments and showcase the continued benefits the buyer receives from working with your organization.

4. Seek Efficiency Improvements: Continually seek ways to improve operational efficiency and reduce costs without sacrificing quality. Implement lean processes, leverage technology, and explore partnerships or collaborations that can streamline operations and

enhance productivity. By finding cost efficiencies, you can maintain or even improve your profit margins while delivering value to the buyer.

5. Upsell and Cross-sell Opportunities: Look for opportunities to offer additional products, services, or upgrades to the buyer that align with their needs and add value. This can help offset any potential margin pressures by increasing the overall revenue generated from the contract. Identify complementary offerings or value-added services that can enhance the buyer's experience and justify any adjustments in pricing.

6. Continuous Monitoring and Adjustment: Regularly review and assess your pricing strategy in light of market dynamics, competitor activities, and customer feedback. Monitor the performance of your pricing model and make necessary adjustments to ensure it remains competitive and profitable. Stay informed about industry trends and changes in buyer expectations to proactively respond to evolving market conditions.

By actively managing your pricing strategy post-award, you can maintain profitability, strengthen customer relationships, and adapt to changing market dynamics. Remember, pricing is not a static component of your business but requires continuous evaluation and optimization to ensure long-term success. By embracing a proactive approach to pricing, you can navigate the challenges of post-award contracts and secure sustainable growth for your business.

Impulsive Pricing

Mistakes in pricing during the bidding process can occur due to various reasons. Here are some common mistakes and the underlying factors that contribute to their occurrence:

1. Reliance on Gut Feeling: One mistake is relying on gut feeling or intuition rather than data-driven analysis. Bidders may fall into the trap of assuming they know the right pricing based on their experience or subjective judgments. This can lead to inaccurate pricing decisions that do not align with market dynamics or customer expectations.

2. Fear of Lower Prices: Some bidders are hesitant to provide lower prices, fearing that it will diminish their profit margins. They may have a fixed mindset that anything below a certain mark-up is not worth their while. This mindset limits their ability to adapt to competitive pricing strategies and explore opportunities to win contracts at lower margins but with the potential for long-term benefits.

3. Lack of Pricing Data Analysis: Bidders who fail to analyze pricing data from previous submissions miss out on valuable insights. Pricing strategies need to evolve over time based on market feedback and performance evaluation. Without analyzing past pricing data and monitoring scorecards, bidders may not have a clear understanding of how to price their offerings to optimize both profitability and competitiveness.

4. Failure to Respond to Changing Market Conditions: Market conditions are dynamic, and failing to respond to these changes can result in pricing inefficiencies. Bidders need to stay updated on industry trends, competitor pricing strategies, and customer expectations. Failure to adapt to changing market conditions can lead to missed opportunities, pricing misalignments, and reduced competitiveness.

5. Limited Pricing Strategy for Non-Tender Work: Bidders may focus solely on pricing strategies for tender-related work and neglect pricing optimization for non-tender projects. This oversight can lead to missed revenue opportunities and suboptimal pricing for other types of engagements. Developing a comprehensive pricing strategy that encompasses all aspects of the business ensures consistent profitability across different project types.

6. Ineffective Value Communication: Bidders may struggle to effectively communicate the value of their offerings, which can result in pricing challenges. Buyers need to understand the unique value they will receive in exchange for the price they pay. Inadequate value communication can undermine the justification for higher prices and make it difficult for bidders to differentiate themselves from competitors.

7. Insufficient Risk Assessment and Mitigation: Failing to assess and address project risks adequately can lead to pricing discrepancies. Buyers are willing to pay a premium for lower perceived risks, and bidders need to transparently address potential challenges and provide robust risk mitigation strategies. Neglecting risk assessment and mitigation can erode buyer confidence and impact the competitiveness of pricing proposals.

These mistakes often stem from a lack of comprehensive market analysis, data-driven decision-making, and a willingness to adapt pricing strategies. Bidders must approach pricing with a strategic mindset, leveraging research insights, market feedback, and collaboration with cross-functional teams to develop effective and optimized pricing strategies for the bidding process.

Developing a strategic and optimized pricing approach in the bidding process comes with its fair share of challenges. Understanding these challenges and leveraging research can further enhance the effectiveness of a pricing strategy. Here are some key challenges and research-backed insights to address them:

1. Pricing Transparency: Buyers increasingly demand transparency in pricing. They expect clear explanations and justifications for the pricing structure proposed. Research conducted by Harvard Business Review suggests that transparency in pricing builds trust and credibility with buyers, increasing the likelihood of winning contracts. Bidders should provide detailed breakdowns of costs, value-added services, and competitive analysis to demonstrate the fairness and competitiveness of their pricing.

2. Competitive Landscape: The bidding process is highly competitive, and bidders need to consider their competitors' pricing strategies. Researching competitor pricing models and analyzing their pricing patterns can provide valuable insights into market positioning and customer expectations. Understanding the pricing landscape allows bidders to differentiate themselves, identify pricing gaps, and make informed decisions to remain competitive.

3. Cost Analysis and Profit Margin Optimization: Accurately assessing costs and optimizing profit margins are critical for sustainable business growth. Conducting thorough cost analysis, including direct and indirect costs, helps bidders determine the minimum price they can offer while ensuring profitability. Research-backed cost optimization techniques, such as lean practices and value engineering, can provide insights into reducing costs without compromising quality, thereby improving profit margins.

4. Pricing Dynamics and Market Trends: Markets are dynamic, and pricing strategies need to adapt to changing trends and demands. Researching market dynamics, including supply and demand factors, customer preferences, and industry trends, helps bidders identify pricing opportunities and adjust their

strategies accordingly. Monitoring market trends through industry reports, economic forecasts, and customer surveys enables bidders to align their pricing with market expectations.

5. Pricing Feedback and Analysis: Collecting feedback from buyers and analyzing past performance is crucial for pricing optimization. Research studies suggest that customer feedback provides valuable insights into pricing perception, competitiveness, and areas for improvement. Bidders should establish feedback mechanisms, conduct post-contract evaluations, and incorporate buyer insights into their pricing strategy to continually refine their approach.

6. Value-Based Pricing: Research shows that value-based pricing, where pricing is aligned with the perceived value delivered to customers, can result in higher profits. Understanding the value drivers for buyers and aligning pricing with the benefits provided can create a compelling value proposition. Market research, customer interviews, and value analysis techniques can help bidders identify the key value drivers and effectively price their offerings.

7. Dynamic Pricing Strategies: Dynamic pricing, based on real-time market conditions and customer behavior, can provide a competitive advantage. Research-backed pricing models, such as price optimization algorithms and revenue management techniques, can help bidders dynamically adjust prices to maximize revenue and profitability. Leveraging data analytics and pricing software can facilitate the implementation of dynamic pricing strategies.

By addressing these challenges and leveraging research-based insights, bidders can develop robust pricing strategies that optimize profitability, enhance competitiveness, and adapt to market dynamics. Pricing should be seen as an opportunity for growth and optimization rather than a random or fixed approach. Continuous learning, adaptation, and the integration of research findings into pricing practices are key to achieving long-term success in the bidding process.

In addition to the challenges and research-backed insights, there are a few more considerations to keep in mind when developing a strategic and optimized pricing approach in the bidding process:

8. Value Communication: Effectively communicating the value proposition of your offering is crucial in pricing. Research indicates that buyers are willing to pay higher prices when they perceive greater value. Bidders should invest time in understanding the specific needs and pain points of the buyer, and articulate how their solution addresses those needs better than competitors. By highlighting unique features, benefits, and value-added services, bidders can justify their pricing and differentiate themselves in the competitive landscape.

9. Risk Assessment and Mitigation: Pricing should take into account the risks associated with the project or contract. Research suggests that buyers are willing to pay a premium for lower perceived risks. Bidders should conduct a thorough risk assessment, considering factors such as project complexity, timeline, and potential challenges. By transparently addressing risks and offering robust risk mitigation strategies, bidders can instill confidence in buyers and justify their pricing.

10. Long-Term Relationship Building: Bidding is not just about winning a single contract; it's about building long-term relationships with buyers. Research shows that customer retention and repeat business have a significant impact on profitability. Bidders should consider the long-term value of the customer relationship when pricing their offerings. Offering competitive prices upfront to establish a strong relationship can lead to future contract extensions and additional opportunities.

11. Continuous Learning and Adaptation: The bidding landscape is constantly evolving, and pricing strategies should evolve with it. Bidders should embrace a mindset of continuous learning and adaptation, staying updated on industry trends, market dynamics, and pricing innovations. Researching and attending industry conferences, engaging in professional networks, and leveraging data analytics can provide valuable insights for pricing optimization and staying ahead of the competition.

12. Collaboration with Cross-Functional Teams: Pricing is not solely the responsibility of the bidding team. Successful pricing strategies require collaboration with cross-functional teams such as sales, marketing, finance, and operations. Research suggests that organizations with strong cross-functional collaboration achieve better pricing outcomes. Bidders should involve relevant stakeholders in pricing discussions to gain diverse perspectives, align strategies, and ensure seamless execution.

By considering these additional aspects and aligning them with the research-backed insights, bidders can develop a comprehensive and effective pricing approach. The bidding process should be seen as an opportunity to demonstrate value, build relationships, and drive profitability. With a strategic and research-informed pricing strategy, bidders can navigate the complexities of the bidding landscape and position themselves for long-term success.

Fixed Forever

Businesses are assuming that prices are fixed and should remain unchanged indefinitely. This misconception can have significant consequences for the long-term success and profitability of a business. Here's why assuming fixed prices is a mistake:

1. Failure to Adapt to Market Dynamics: Markets are dynamic and constantly evolving. Customer preferences, demand levels, and competitive landscapes can change over time. If a business assumes that its pricing strategy will remain effective without any adjustments, it may find itself out of touch with the market. This can result in lost opportunities, decreased market share, and diminished profitability. Adapting prices to reflect changing market conditions is crucial for remaining competitive and meeting customer expectations.

2. Missed Revenue Opportunities: Fixed prices can prevent businesses from capitalizing on revenue opportunities. By not regularly evaluating and adjusting prices, businesses may fail to capture the full value of their offerings. If market demand for a product or service increases, maintaining fixed prices means leaving potential revenue on the table. On the other hand, if demand decreases, fixed prices may result in overpricing and hinder sales. Flexibility in pricing allows businesses to optimize revenue and maximize their market potential.

3. Inability to Respond to Competitive Pressures: Competitors play a vital role in shaping market dynamics. If a business assumes fixed prices, it may struggle to respond effectively to pricing strategies employed by competitors. If a competitor lowers prices, a business with fixed prices may lose customers who are attracted by the lower-priced alternative. By failing to adjust prices in response to competitive pressures, a business risks losing its competitive advantage and market position.

4. Value Perception and Customer Expectations: Fixed prices can impact how customers perceive the value of a product or service. If prices remain the same while competitors offer lower prices or enhanced value, customers may perceive the business as overpriced or less competitive. This can lead to a decline in customer loyalty and decreased sales. Regularly evaluating and adjusting prices helps ensure that the perceived value aligns with customer expectations and market conditions.

5. Cost and Profitability Considerations: Over time, costs of production, raw materials, labor, and other inputs may fluctuate. If a business assumes fixed prices, it may not account for these changes, potentially eroding profit margins. Regularly reviewing and adjusting prices based on cost considerations is crucial for maintaining profitability and ensuring that prices adequately reflect the business's cost structure.

By staying attuned to market dynamics and being willing to adjust prices accordingly, businesses can position themselves for sustained success, increased profitability, and enhanced customer satisfaction.

Here are some key reasons why this mistake occurs:

1. Ignoring Market Insights: Many businesses overlook the importance of conducting thorough market research. Without a clear understanding of market trends, customer preferences, and competitor pricing strategies, businesses are more likely to set prices based on assumptions or internal preferences rather than market realities. This can lead to pricing that is out of touch with customer expectations and fails to capture market share.

2. Overemphasis on Cost: Some businesses rely solely on cost-based pricing, setting prices based on production or operational costs without considering market demand or competitive positioning. While it's important to ensure profitability, pricing decisions

should also consider factors such as value proposition, customer perception, and willingness to pay. Overemphasizing cost can result in missed opportunities to capture additional value from customers and differentiate from competitors.

3. Failure to Differentiate: Another common mistake is failing to differentiate the value proposition and pricing strategy from competitors. Without a unique selling proposition or a clear value differentiation, businesses may resort to competing solely on price. This often leads to price wars, eroding profit margins and devaluing the offering in the eyes of customers. It's essential to identify and communicate the unique benefits and value customers will receive, justifying a higher price point.

4. Lack of Pricing Flexibility: Businesses that stick rigidly to a single pricing model or fail to adapt to changing market conditions can miss out on opportunities or struggle to remain competitive. Pricing flexibility is key to responding to shifts in customer demand, market trends, and competitive pressures. It's important to regularly review and adjust pricing strategies to align with evolving market dynamics and maintain a competitive edge.

5. Failure to Continuously Monitor Competitors: Failing to keep a close eye on competitors' pricing strategies can be detrimental. Pricing decisions should be informed by a thorough understanding of competitor offerings, pricing models, and value propositions. By continuously monitoring the market, businesses can identify gaps, opportunities, and emerging pricing trends. This enables them to make informed pricing decisions and respond effectively to competitor moves.

6. Inadequate Customer Feedback: Businesses that don't actively seek customer feedback on pricing and value perception miss valuable insights. Customer feedback can highlight areas where pricing may be

too high or too low, shed light on competitors' pricing strategies, and provide input on the overall value proposition. By soliciting and incorporating customer feedback, businesses can refine their pricing strategy and better meet customer needs.

Developing an effective pricing strategy is crucial for business success. It requires careful analysis, thoughtful consideration of market dynamics, and a deep understanding of customer preferences. Here are the key steps to create an amazing pricing strategy:

1. Market Research: Begin by conducting thorough market research to gain insights into industry trends, competitor pricing strategies, and customer expectations. This will help you identify market gaps and opportunities for differentiation.

2. Customer Segmentation: Segment your target market based on specific customer profiles, needs, and preferences. This allows you to tailor your pricing approach to different customer segments, offering personalized value propositions.

3. Value Proposition: Clearly define your unique value proposition and articulate the benefits customers will receive from your product or service. Highlight the value drivers that set you apart from competitors and justify your pricing.

4. Cost Analysis: Conduct a comprehensive cost analysis to understand your cost structure and identify areas for efficiency improvement. This includes evaluating direct costs, overhead expenses, and operational efficiencies to optimize your pricing and profitability.

5. Pricing Model Selection: Choose an appropriate pricing model that aligns with your business goals and customer expectations. Consider options such as cost-plus pricing, value-based pricing, or competitive pricing based on market benchmarks.

6.   Competitive Analysis: Analyze your competitors' pricing strategies and positioning to identify gaps and opportunities. Determine how you can differentiate your offering through pricing, whether it's by offering premium features or providing cost-effective alternatives.

7.   Pricing Tiers and Bundles: Develop pricing tiers or bundled offerings that cater to different customer segments and their varying needs. This allows you to capture additional value from customers willing to pay for enhanced features or services.

8.   Test and Refine: Implement your pricing strategy on a small scale and gather feedback from customers. Continuously monitor and analyze results, making adjustments as necessary to optimize your pricing approach.

9.   Pricing Flexibility: Remain flexible and responsive to changing market conditions. Regularly reassess your pricing strategy and adapt it to evolving customer demands, competitive landscape, and cost dynamics.

10. Value Communication: Effectively communicate the value customers will receive at each pricing level. Highlight the benefits, features, and outcomes that make your offering compelling and demonstrate why it's worth the price.

11. Customer Feedback: Solicit feedback from customers on their perception of your pricing and value proposition. Use this feedback to refine your strategy and address any concerns or objections.

12. Monitor Competitor Pricing: Continuously monitor your competitors' pricing strategies and adjust your pricing accordingly. Stay informed about market trends and ensure your pricing remains competitive while maintaining profitability.

By following these steps, you can create an amazing pricing strategy that optimizes profitability, meets customer needs, and positions your business for success in the marketplace. Remember, pricing is a dynamic process that requires ongoing evaluation and adaptation to stay ahead of the competition and maximize your revenue potential.

Repeat References

Using the same references for every bid is a common and detrimental mistake made by many bidders. It not only limits their ability to provide compelling and tailored responses but also fails to showcase their versatility and adaptability. Let's explore the consequences of this mistake and the benefits of diversifying the range of references used in tender submissions.

When bidders rely on the same references for each bid, they risk offering information that may not directly address the specific needs outlined in the tender documents. This lack of relevance undermines the strength of their response and diminishes their chances of winning the contract. Tailoring the references to match the specific requirements of each bid allows bidders to demonstrate their deep understanding of the buyer's needs and increase their competitiveness.

Moreover, repeating the same references in every bid fails to showcase a bidder's growth and progress over time. It suggests a lack of new experiences, recent successes, and the ability to adapt to evolving market demands. By regularly updating and diversifying the references, bidders can demonstrate their ongoing commitment to professional development, their ability to handle diverse projects, and their capacity to deliver innovative solutions. This dynamic approach signals to buyers that the bidder is forward-thinking and continuously strives for improvement.

Using the same references also restricts a bidder's ability to showcase their creativity and innovative approaches. Each project and client is unique, and by drawing on a broader range of references, bidders can demonstrate their adaptability and resourcefulness. Diverse references offer a wealth of experiences and insights that can be leveraged to present unique solutions and demonstrate a comprehensive understanding of the buyer's challenges. This flexibility sets bidders apart from their competitors and enhances their chances of success.

Building a robust and diverse portfolio of references enhances a bidder's credibility and fosters trust with potential buyers. A varied set of references showcases the bidder's expertise across different industries, sectors, and project scopes. It demonstrates a track record of successful collaborations and instills confidence in the buyer that the bidder can meet their unique requirements. Having a wide range of references allows bidders to establish a strong reputation and position themselves as reliable and capable partners.

Finally, utilizing a variety of references enables bidders to demonstrate their ability to tackle different challenges and work with various clients. Each reference offers a different perspective, illustrating the bidder's versatility and adaptability to different project contexts. This showcases the bidder's capacity to handle diverse situations, overcome obstacles, and deliver exceptional results. Buyers are more likely to trust bidders who have a proven track record of success in a range of scenarios.

By avoiding the mistake of using the same references repeatedly, bidders can unlock numerous benefits. Diversifying the range of references allows for tailored and relevant responses, highlights growth and adaptability, fosters innovation, strengthens credibility, and showcases versatility. By investing time and effort in maintaining a comprehensive and up-to-date portfolio of references, bidders position themselves as strong contenders in the competitive tendering landscape.

Furthermore, the use of varied references demonstrates a bidder's commitment to building strong relationships and maintaining a network of satisfied clients and partners. By showcasing a range of references from different projects, industries, and stakeholders, bidders signal their ability to collaborate effectively and deliver value across various contexts. This not only enhances their reputation but also increases their chances of securing future contracts through positive word-of-mouth referrals and recommendations.

Another significant advantage of diversifying references is the ability to highlight specific skills, expertise, and capabilities that align with the requirements of each bid. Different projects may require different sets of skills or specialized knowledge, and by drawing on a diverse range of references, bidders can effectively showcase their proficiency in specific areas. This tailored approach not only enhances the relevance of their bid but also positions them as experts in their field, capable of delivering exceptional results.

Moreover, utilizing a variety of references allows bidders to demonstrate their understanding of industry trends, best practices, and emerging technologies. By referencing projects that incorporate the latest innovations and methodologies, bidders can convey their commitment to staying ahead of the curve and their ability to leverage cutting-edge solutions. This demonstrates their capacity to bring fresh perspectives and deliver outcomes that are aligned with industry standards and expectations.

It is important to note that while diversifying references is crucial, maintaining the quality and accuracy of the information provided is equally essential. Bidders should ensure that the references chosen are reliable, relevant, and up to date. They should be prepared to provide supporting documentation and testimonials, if necessary, to validate their claims and instill confidence in the buyer's decision-making process.

The strategic use of references is a critical aspect of successful bidding. One of the biggest mistakes bidders can make is relying on the same set of references for every bid, without considering the specific requirements and nuances of each opportunity. This approach not only limits the bidder's ability to provide tailored responses but also undermines their credibility and reduces their chances of securing contracts.

When bidders recycle the same references, it sends a message that they are not actively engaged in their industry or that they lack the breadth of experience necessary to handle diverse projects. This lack of adaptability and innovation can be a red flag for buyers, who are seeking partners that can bring fresh insights, creative solutions, and a track record of success in similar contexts.

By diversifying references, bidders demonstrate their commitment to building a robust network of satisfied clients, collaborators, and industry partners. This diverse range of references serves as a testament to their ability to establish and maintain positive relationships, work effectively with different stakeholders, and deliver value across various projects and industries. Buyers are more likely to be impressed by a bidder who can showcase a broad spectrum of references, as it showcases their versatility and adaptability.

In addition to signaling adaptability, diversified references enable bidders to highlight specific skills, expertise, and capabilities that align with the requirements of each bid. Different projects may call for unique skill sets or specialized knowledge, and by leveraging a varied range of references, bidders can demonstrate their proficiency in specific areas. This targeted approach not only enhances the relevance of their bid but also positions them as experts in their field, capable of delivering exceptional results.

Furthermore, utilizing a variety of references allows bidders to showcase their understanding of industry trends, best practices, and emerging technologies. By referencing projects that incorporate the latest innovations and methodologies, bidders can demonstrate their commitment to staying ahead of the curve and their ability to leverage cutting-edge solutions. This demonstrates their capacity to bring fresh perspectives and deliver outcomes that are aligned with industry standards and expectations.

It is crucial to note that while diversifying references is important, maintaining the quality and accuracy of the information provided is equally essential. Bidders should ensure that the references chosen are reliable, relevant, and up to date. They should be prepared to provide supporting documentation, testimonials, or case studies to substantiate their claims and

The mistake of using the same references for each bid can significantly hinder a bidder's chances of success. By diversifying the range of references, bidders can create tailored and compelling responses, showcase their growth and adaptability, foster innovation, strengthen credibility, and highlight their versatility and expertise. Investing time and effort into building a comprehensive portfolio of diverse references allows bidders to position themselves as highly competitive and reliable partners in the tendering process. By leveraging a variety of references effectively, bidders can enhance their chances of securing contracts and achieving long-term success in the marketplace.

Frozen

Failing to create new case studies regularly is a critical mistake that can significantly impact a bidder's success in the bidding process. Case studies play a crucial role in showcasing a bidder's capabilities, expertise, and track record of success. By relying on the same outdated case studies or failing to produce new ones, bidders miss out on opportunities to highlight their recent accomplishments, demonstrate their adaptability, and differentiate themselves from competitors.

Case studies serve as powerful tools for building credibility and trust with potential clients. They provide tangible evidence of a bidder's ability to deliver results, solve complex problems, and meet the unique needs of clients. However, relying on the same case studies repeatedly can give the impression that a bidder is stagnant or lacks recent success stories to showcase. This can raise doubts in the minds of buyers, who are looking for partners that can demonstrate ongoing growth, innovation, and the capacity to meet evolving challenges.

Creating new case studies regularly is a proactive approach that showcases a bidder's commitment to continuous improvement and staying at the forefront of their industry. It allows bidders to demonstrate their ability to adapt to changing market conditions, incorporate new technologies or methodologies, and deliver value in diverse contexts. By presenting a portfolio of recent and varied case studies, bidders can convey their relevance, relevance, and competitiveness in the market.

Moreover, producing new case studies regularly provides bidders with the opportunity to showcase their expertise in specific industries, project types, or problem-solving approaches. Different bids may require different areas of expertise or highlight specific challenges that can be addressed through relevant case studies. By having a diverse range of case studies, bidders can tailor their responses to align with the specific needs and requirements of each bid, increasing their chances of success.

Additionally, creating new case studies fosters internal growth and learning within the bidding organization. It encourages teams to reflect on their past projects, identify lessons learned, and document best practices. This not only enhances the bidding process but also creates a culture of continuous improvement, where employees are encouraged to innovate, explore new solutions, and deliver exceptional results.

To ensure the effectiveness of case studies, bidders should focus on capturing the key elements of each project, including the background, challenges faced, approach taken, solutions implemented, and measurable outcomes achieved. They should highlight the specific value added to the client's organization and quantify the benefits realized. Visual elements such as graphs, charts, or images can be used to enhance the presentation of data and make the case study more engaging and memorable.

Additionally, research supports the importance of regularly creating new case studies in the bidding process. Studies have shown that bidders who consistently update their case studies and demonstrate a track record of successful projects are more likely to win contracts and achieve higher levels of client satisfaction. This highlights the significance of continuously refreshing and expanding your portfolio of case studies.

One study conducted by a reputable research group analyzed the bidding practices of several companies across different industries. The findings revealed a clear correlation between the frequency of updating case studies and bidding success. Companies that regularly created new case studies and tailored them to align with bid requirements had a significantly higher win rate compared to those who relied on outdated or generic case studies.

Furthermore, the study emphasized the importance of leveraging case studies as marketing and sales tools beyond the bidding process. Effective case studies can be repurposed to support marketing campaigns, sales presentations, and client testimonials. By showcasing real-world examples of successful projects, businesses can strengthen their brand reputation, attract new clients, and differentiate themselves from competitors.

Another research study explored the impact of case studies on client decision-making. The study found that clients heavily rely on case studies to evaluate a bidder's capabilities and assess their fit for a particular project. Clients perceive case studies as tangible evidence of a bidder's expertise, reliability, and ability to deliver results. Therefore, bidders who regularly update their case studies not only demonstrate their commitment to excellence but also instill confidence in potential clients.

In light of these research findings, it is evident that failing to create new case studies regularly can be a costly mistake. It not only limits a bidder's success in the bidding process but also hinders their overall growth and market positioning. Bidders must prioritize the continuous development of fresh, compelling case studies that showcase their recent accomplishments, highlight their unique value proposition, and address specific client needs.

To effectively create new case studies, bidders should establish a systematic approach that includes regular project evaluation, documentation, and collaboration with clients to gather testimonials and measurable outcomes. They should also consider utilizing multimedia formats, such as videos or interactive presentations, to enhance the visual appeal and engagement of their case studies.

The significance of regularly creating new case studies cannot be overstated. By doing so, bidders can demonstrate their ongoing growth, relevance, and expertise, and significantly increase their chances of winning contracts. Incorporating research-backed strategies and best practices ensures that case studies are compelling, tailored, and impactful. As bidders continue to prioritize the development of fresh case studies, they position themselves as industry leaders and trusted partners in the eyes of clients.

Failing to create new case studies regularly is a significant mistake that can hinder a bidder's success in the bidding process. By proactively developing and showcasing a diverse range of case studies, bidders can demonstrate their ongoing growth, relevance, and expertise. Creating new case studies not only enhances credibility and trust but also allows for tailored responses to specific bid requirements. It fosters internal learning and improvement, positioning the bidding organization as a dynamic and competitive player in the market. By recognizing the importance of case studies and investing in their regular creation, bidders can significantly enhance their chances of securing contracts and achieving long-term success.

Invalidating Content

Invalidating good evidence is a common and detrimental mistake that many bidders make in the tendering process. While they may possess an impressive repository of project examples and case studies, their failure to effectively connect them to the specific requirements and needs of the buyer or procurement team undermines the strength of their bid. This often occurs when bidders resort to copy-pasting information without carefully fine-tuning and tailoring it to the unique demands of each bid, resulting in diminished scores or outright rejection.

Consider a scenario where a bidder has a case study showcasing their success in implementing a large-scale IT project for a government agency. However, in their next bid for a healthcare contract, they simply include the same case study without highlighting the relevant aspects that demonstrate their capability to meet the specific needs of the healthcare sector. The procurement team, assessing the bid, may perceive the evidence as irrelevant or not directly applicable to their requirements, leading to a significant reduction in points awarded.

To avoid this mistake, bidders must invest the necessary time and effort to connect their evidence to the bid's specific requirements. They should carefully analyze the buyer's expectations, evaluate the key criteria outlined in the bid, and identify the relevant aspects of their project examples and case studies that address these requirements. This may involve extracting specific accomplishments, methodologies, or outcomes from their past projects and explicitly demonstrating how they align with the buyer's needs.

For example, let's consider a construction company bidding for a contract to build a hospital. The company has a case study detailing their successful completion of a similar project, constructing a school. While the project management and execution skills showcased in the school construction case study are relevant to the hospital project, the bidder must go a step further. They should highlight specific aspects, such as their experience in working with healthcare regulations, their understanding of specialized infrastructure requirements, or their expertise in managing complex stakeholder relationships in a healthcare environment. By emphasizing these relevant elements, the bidder can strengthen their case and demonstrate their suitability for the hospital construction contract.

In situations where bidders struggle to find directly applicable project examples, they can employ creative approaches to establish relevancy. For instance, they could focus on the expertise and experience of individual team members who have worked on projects similar to the bid's requirements. By crafting case studies that showcase the accomplishments and contributions of these team members, bidders can effectively demonstrate their capabilities and expertise, even if the organization as a whole lacks a direct case study.

For example, a software development company bidding for a contract to develop a customized e-commerce platform may lack a specific case study for a similar project. However, they can create a case study centered around a key team member who successfully delivered a complex and customized software solution for a different industry. By highlighting the individual's technical skills, problem-solving abilities, and project management expertise, the bidder can demonstrate their competence and relevance to the e-commerce project, even without an exact matching case study.

Avoiding the mistake of invalidating good evidence requires bidders to invest time and effort in connecting their project examples and case studies to the specific requirements of each bid. By carefully analyzing the buyer's needs, tailoring the evidence to highlight relevant aspects, and considering creative approaches such as showcasing individual team member expertise, bidders can strengthen their bid and increase their chances of success.

In addition to avoiding the mistake of invalidating good evidence, bidders should also consider the broader implications and consequences of this error. Failing to effectively connect their evidence to bid requirements can have significant ramifications for their overall bid strategy and success rate.

One of the key implications is a loss of credibility and trust from the buyer or procurement team. When bidders submit generic or irrelevant evidence, it raises doubts about their understanding of the project's specific needs and their ability to deliver the desired outcomes. Buyers want assurance that the bidder has the necessary expertise and experience to meet their requirements, and failing to provide relevant evidence can erode confidence in the bidder's capabilities.

Moreover, invalidating good evidence can result in missed opportunities for differentiation and competitive advantage. Bidders who effectively align their evidence with bid requirements have a chance to showcase their unique strengths, specialized knowledge, and past successes that directly relate to the project at hand. By leveraging these differentiators, bidders can position themselves as the most suitable and compelling choice for the contract. However, when evidence is not properly connected, bidders miss out on the opportunity to stand out and differentiate themselves from competitors.

Another consequence of invalidating good evidence is a missed opportunity for continuous improvement and learning. By neglecting to analyze and adapt their case studies and project examples for each bid, bidders fail to capture valuable insights and lessons learned from their previous experiences. Each bid presents an opportunity to refine and enhance their evidence, ensuring that it reflects the bidder's evolving expertise and the changing needs of the market. Without this iterative approach, bidders may stagnate and miss out on valuable growth and development opportunities.

To avoid the pitfalls of invalidating good evidence, bidders should adopt a proactive and strategic approach to their case study and project example management. This includes regularly reviewing and updating their evidence library to reflect recent accomplishments, client feedback, and industry trends. Bidders should also invest in conducting thorough research on each bid to understand the specific requirements and tailor their evidence accordingly. By taking these steps, bidders can ensure that their evidence remains relevant, compelling, and aligned with the buyer's expectations.

Failing to connect evidence to bid requirements can have significant implications for bidders. It undermines credibility, limits opportunities for differentiation, and hinders continuous improvement. Bidders should prioritize the alignment of their evidence with bid requirements, taking a strategic and iterative approach to their case study and project example management. By doing so, bidders can enhance their chances of success, build trust with buyers, and position themselves as top contenders in the competitive bidding landscape.

Fear

One of the most significant mistakes that bidders can make is allowing fear to prevent them from seeking evidence and involving their team members and stakeholders in the bidding process. This fear may stem from concerns about appearing inexperienced or the fear of asking for help. However, it is crucial to recognize that collaboration and the exchange of information are vital for successful bidding.

When working with other organizations and professionals, there is a shared goal of achieving success in the bidding process. These individuals and entities have unique insights, expertise, and access to valuable information that can significantly enhance the quality of tender proposals. By treating them as integral team members and actively involving them, bidders can tap into a wealth of knowledge and experience that can elevate their bids to a new level.

Our approach to bidding goes beyond just being bid writers. We recognize the value of business specialists who have established connections within each organization and possess industry-specific knowledge. These individuals take charge of business growth and successful bidding by actively seeking out information and leveraging the expertise of stakeholders. We refer to them as "CIP Bidders," as they continuously strive for improvement and excellence in the bidding process.

Incorporating the perspectives of all stakeholders is essential. This includes sub-contractors, vendors, suppliers, and any other party involved in the project. By forging strong connections and fostering open communication, bidders can collaborate effectively, gather relevant information, and gain a deeper understanding of project requirements. Each interaction and piece of data obtained from stakeholders can provide valuable insights and contribute to strengthening the overall company profile.

Overcoming the fear of asking for evidence and involving team members and stakeholders requires a shift in mindset. It requires recognizing that collaboration is not a sign of weakness, but rather a strategic approach to accessing a wider range of expertise and perspectives. By creating a culture of open communication and trust, bidders can foster an environment where stakeholders feel comfortable sharing their insights and providing the evidence needed to enhance tender proposals.

Additionally, seeking evidence and involving stakeholders should be seen as an ongoing process. It is not a one-time event but a continuous effort to gather information, refine strategies, and improve bidding outcomes. By embracing a culture of continuous improvement, bidders can create an environment where feedback is valued, and lessons learned from previous bids are used to enhance future ones.

Collaboration, open communication, and a commitment to continuous improvement are essential elements in harnessing the collective knowledge and expertise within the bidding team and stakeholder network. By actively seeking input, insights, and evidence, bidders can develop stronger, more informed tender proposals that stand out in the competitive bidding landscape.

Furthermore, the benefits of seeking evidence and involving team members and stakeholders extend beyond the immediate bidding process. By actively engaging with stakeholders and tapping into their expertise, bidders can cultivate stronger relationships and foster a sense of ownership and collaboration. This not only enhances the quality of tender proposals but also lays the foundation for successful project execution and long-term partnerships.

When bidders embrace the practice of involving stakeholders, they create an environment of inclusivity and shared responsibility. Stakeholders become invested in the bidding process and are more likely to provide valuable insights, offer support, and contribute to the overall success of the project. This collaborative approach not only strengthens the bidding team but also builds trust and credibility with the client.

In addition, involving stakeholders allows for a broader perspective on the project. Each stakeholder brings their unique knowledge, experience, and industry insights, which can uncover innovative solutions, identify potential risks, and address any challenges that may arise during the bidding process. By leveraging this collective wisdom, bidders can enhance the competitiveness and strategic positioning of their tender proposals.

Furthermore, involving stakeholders ensures that all relevant information is considered and incorporated into the bidding strategy. Different perspectives and expertise can shed light on critical aspects such as budgeting, risk assessment, compliance requirements, and project feasibility. This comprehensive approach demonstrates thoroughness, professionalism, and a commitment to delivering high-quality outcomes.

However, it is essential to approach the process of involving stakeholders with clarity and structure. Clear communication channels, defined roles and responsibilities, and effective project management frameworks are key to ensuring that information flows smoothly and that stakeholders are engaged in a meaningful way. Regular meetings, collaborative workshops, and open dialogue provide opportunities for stakeholders to contribute their insights, share information, and address any concerns or questions.

The mistake of being too scared to ask for evidence and involving team members and stakeholders can hinder the bidding process and limit the potential for success. By overcoming this fear and actively involving stakeholders, bidders can unlock a wealth of expertise, improve the quality of tender proposals, foster collaboration, and build stronger relationships. This approach not only enhances the bidding process but also sets the stage for successful project execution and long-term business growth.

Performance Struggles

Performance measurement is a critical aspect of achieving continuous improvement and success in the bidding process. It is not only applicable to bidders but holds true for all businesses. Failing to measure performance can result in a lack of awareness or oversight regarding important indicators, hindering the ability to make informed decisions and drive progress.

While performance measurement is crucial for business success, there are several common mistakes that organizations may make when implementing this practice:

1. Lack of clarity on goals and metrics: One mistake is not clearly defining the goals and metrics that align with the business strategy. Without a clear understanding of what to measure and why, organizations may end up tracking irrelevant or misaligned metrics that do not provide meaningful insights.

2. Inadequate data collection and analysis: Another mistake is failing to collect and analyze relevant data effectively. Organizations may struggle with capturing accurate and comprehensive performance data, leading to incomplete or inaccurate assessments. Additionally, without proper analysis and interpretation of the data, valuable insights may be missed, and opportunities for improvement may go unnoticed.

3. Overemphasis on lagging indicators: Relying solely on lagging indicators, such as past performance metrics, can be a mistake. While these indicators provide historical information, they do not provide timely insights for proactive decision-making. Organizations should also focus on leading indicators that can help predict future performance and guide improvement efforts.

4. Failure to align performance measurement with strategy: Organizations may make the mistake of not

aligning performance measurement with their overall business strategy. It is essential to ensure that the metrics being tracked directly contribute to the organization's strategic objectives. Without this alignment, organizations may waste resources on measuring irrelevant or conflicting metrics.

5. Neglecting the importance of context: Performance measurement without considering the broader context can be misleading. Organizations must understand the external factors, market conditions, and industry benchmarks that influence performance. Failing to consider these factors can lead to unrealistic expectations or misinterpretation of performance data.

6. Lack of action and follow-through: One of the biggest mistakes is collecting performance data without taking appropriate action based on the insights gained. Organizations may identify areas for improvement but fail to follow through with implementing changes or addressing underlying issues. Without action, performance measurement becomes a futile exercise.

To avoid these mistakes, organizations should invest time and resources in designing a robust performance measurement framework. This involves clearly defining goals, selecting relevant metrics, establishing data collection processes, conducting regular analysis, and most importantly, using the insights gained to drive meaningful improvements in business performance. Additionally, organizations should foster a culture of continuous improvement, where performance measurement is embraced as a catalyst for growth and innovation.

The irony is that measuring performance is not a complex or daunting task. At its core, it simply involves recording and tracking relevant data and metrics related to business activities and processes. This can include quantifiable measures such as the number of orders processed or delivered on time, the response time to customer inquiries, or the percentage of successful bid submissions. By diligently capturing this information, businesses gain valuable insights that can be used to assess performance, identify areas for improvement, and make data-driven decisions.

One of the primary benefits of performance measurement is gaining better control and visibility into business operations. By tracking key performance indicators (KPIs), bidders can assess their efficiency, productivity, and overall performance. This enables them to identify bottlenecks, inefficiencies, or areas of underperformance that may be negatively impacting the bidding process. Armed with this information, businesses can implement targeted strategies and initiatives to address these issues and optimize their performance.

Moreover, performance measurement plays a crucial role in risk management. By monitoring performance metrics, businesses can proactively identify potential risks or deviations from desired outcomes. For example, if the response time to customer inquiries starts to increase, it may indicate a breakdown in communication or resource constraints that could affect the bidding process. By recognizing these early warning signs, businesses can take corrective action to mitigate risks and ensure smooth operations.

Performance measurement also fosters a culture of continuous improvement. By analyzing performance data over time, businesses can identify trends, patterns, and opportunities for enhancement. For instance, if the data reveals a consistently high percentage of successful bid submissions, it may indicate effective bidding strategies and provide valuable insights into what works well. On the other hand, if there is a decline in success rates, it prompts a closer examination of the bidding process to identify areas that need improvement.

To effectively implement performance measurement, businesses should establish a structured approach. This involves clearly defining the relevant performance metrics and ensuring that the necessary data is consistently captured and recorded. The data can be collected through various methods, such as automated systems, manual tracking, or customer feedback. Regular analysis and reporting of the performance data are crucial to identify trends, track progress, and make informed decisions.

It is worth noting that performance measurement is not a one-time exercise but an ongoing process. Regularly reviewing and analyzing performance data allows businesses to adapt and adjust strategies, seize opportunities for improvement, and ensure that they remain competitive in the bidding process. By embracing a culture of continuous improvement and utilizing performance measurement as a tool for growth, businesses can enhance their bidding performance, increase their success rates, and drive long-term success.

Performance measurement is an essential component of successful bidding and overall business growth. It provides valuable insights into operational efficiency, risk management, and areas for improvement. By diligently tracking and analyzing performance metrics, businesses can make informed decisions, optimize their bidding strategies, and foster a culture of continuous improvement. Embracing performance measurement as a fundamental practice enables businesses to enhance their competitiveness, achieve better results, and drive long-term success in the dynamic bidding landscape.

Negative Influence

Research conducted by Barbara Fredrickson, a leading expert in positive psychology, has shown that negative emotions narrow individuals' focus and hinder cognitive flexibility, creativity, and problem-solving abilities. This suggests that exposure to negative content can impair a bidder's ability to think critically, generate innovative ideas, and effectively respond to challenges during the bidding process.

Furthermore, a study published in the Journal of Applied Psychology by Kristin Byron and colleagues explored the impact of workplace negativity on employee performance. The findings revealed that negative work environments were associated with decreased job satisfaction, lower motivation, and reduced productivity. These outcomes can translate to the bidding context, where negativity can undermine a bidder's drive, enthusiasm, and overall performance.

Additionally, research on team dynamics and performance highlights the importance of a positive work environment. A study published in the Journal of Organizational Behavior by Emily Heaphy and Marcial Losada found that high-performing teams had a significantly higher ratio of positive to negative interactions compared to low-performing teams. This suggests that a positive team culture, characterized by constructive communication and supportive relationships, is crucial for achieving optimal performance.

While direct research on negativity in the bidding process is limited, these studies provide insights into the broader impact of negative content on individual and team performance. By extrapolating these findings, it is reasonable to conclude that negative content can hinder a bidder's motivation, productivity, and ability to form positive relationships with clients.

To mitigate the negative effects of content, research on positive psychology emphasizes the importance of cultivating positive emotions, such as joy, gratitude, and optimism. Studies have shown that positive emotions broaden individuals' cognitive capacities, enhance problem-solving abilities, and improve overall well-being.

Creating a positive environment is crucial for maintaining high productivity and motivation in the bidding process. Negative content and pessimistic attitudes can hinder a bidder's performance and overall success. However, top bidders understand the importance of surrounding themselves with positive information and cultivating an optimistic mindset.

Negative content can come in various forms, such as discouraging feedback, pessimistic news, or toxic conversations. Exposing oneself to such negativity can have a detrimental impact on motivation, confidence, and creativity. It can lead to a sense of self-doubt, decreased productivity, and even burnout.

To counteract the negative influences, top bidders actively seek out positive information and surround themselves with uplifting content. They understand that positive reinforcement and encouragement are vital for maintaining high levels of motivation and inspiration. By engaging with positive industry news, success stories, and personal development resources, bidders can fuel their enthusiasm and stay focused on their goals.

Moreover, top bidders proactively manage their mindset by practicing positive self-talk and visualization techniques. They consciously choose to focus on their strengths, achievements, and the potential for growth. This optimistic mindset enables them to overcome challenges, embrace learning opportunities, and maintain a high level of confidence throughout the bidding process.

In my own team, we prioritize creating a positive environment. We foster an atmosphere of support, collaboration, and celebration of successes. We recognize that positive energy and encouragement are contagious, spreading throughout the team and elevating everyone's performance.

By immersing ourselves in positive content and maintaining an optimistic mindset, we enhance our productivity, creativity, and overall effectiveness. We understand that positivity is not just a fleeting mood but a deliberate choice that fuels our success.

The negative content can significantly impact a bidder's performance and motivation. Top bidders actively counteract this by seeking out positive information, cultivating an optimistic mindset, and surrounding themselves with supportive environments. By embracing positivity, bidders can maintain high productivity, overcome challenges, and achieve their goals in the bidding process.

In addition to the impact of negative content, it's important to recognize the broader consequences it can have on a bidder's overall performance and the bidding process as a whole. When negativity permeates the bidding environment, it can create a ripple effect that extends beyond the individual bidder.

Negative content not only affects the mindset and motivation of the bidder but can also influence the dynamics within the team. When team members are exposed to pessimistic attitudes or discouraging information, it can erode their enthusiasm, collaboration, and overall effectiveness. This can lead to a decline in team morale, communication breakdowns, and reduced productivity.

Furthermore, negative content can also impact relationships with clients and stakeholders. When bidders are immersed in negativity, it can overshadow their ability to build strong, positive connections with potential clients. Negative mindsets can inadvertently project onto interactions, hindering effective communication and rapport building. This can ultimately impact the bidder's success in securing contracts and maintaining long-term client relationships.

To counteract these negative effects, it is essential for bidders to actively cultivate a positive environment. This involves not only filtering out negative content but also actively seeking out positive and inspiring sources of information. Bidders can leverage industry publications, success stories, and motivational resources to stay informed and inspired.

Creating a supportive and positive team culture is equally important. Bidders can foster an environment that encourages open communication, constructive feedback, and recognition of achievements. Celebrating successes, big or small, helps to reinforce a positive mindset and encourages continuous improvement.

Additionally, implementing strategies to manage stress and maintain work-life balance can contribute to a positive environment. Bidders should prioritize self-care, engage in activities that bring joy and relaxation, and establish boundaries to prevent burnout.

By consciously cultivating a positive environment, bidders can enhance their own performance, boost team morale, and foster strong relationships with clients. It creates a virtuous cycle where positivity fuels motivation, productivity, and success in the bidding process.

By actively seeking out positive information, fostering a supportive team culture, and prioritizing self-care, bidders can counteract the negative effects and create an environment that breeds motivation, productivity, and success.

Conflicts

Procurement and bidding are two critical components of the business landscape, each with its unique set of challenges and considerations. While procurement specialists excel in managing the sourcing and acquisition process, bidders and tender management professionals bring a distinct perspective and expertise to the table. Understanding the differences between these roles is crucial in developing a comprehensive understanding of tender management and winning contracts.

Here are some examples that illustrate the differences between procurement and bidding professionals:

1. Evaluation Perspective:

    o   Procurement Professional: A procurement professional evaluates supplier proposals based on predetermined criteria such as cost, quality, and compliance. Their focus is on selecting the supplier that offers the best overall value for the organization.

    o   Bidding Professional: A bidding professional, on the other hand, prepares and submits proposals that align with the buyer's requirements. They strategically position their offering to highlight unique strengths, competitive advantages, and value-added benefits to stand out from other bidders.

2. Negotiation Approach:

    o   Procurement Professional: Procurement professionals negotiate contract terms and conditions to ensure favorable terms for their organization. Their goal is to secure the most advantageous agreement in terms of pricing, delivery, and contractual obligations.

    o   Bidding Professional: Bidding professionals focus on crafting compelling proposals that effectively communicate the value they bring to the table. While they may engage in negotiations, their primary objective is to showcase their capabilities and differentiate themselves from competitors.

3. Risk Management:

    o Procurement Professional: Procurement professionals assess supplier risks and implement risk mitigation strategies to safeguard their organization's interests. They conduct due diligence, evaluate supplier financial stability, and ensure compliance with legal and regulatory requirements.

    o Bidding Professional: Bidding professionals analyze project risks and develop strategies to mitigate them in their proposals. They showcase their expertise in managing risks specific to the project, addressing potential challenges, and providing solutions that inspire confidence in the buyer.

4. Relationship Building:

    o Procurement Professional: Procurement professionals establish and maintain relationships with suppliers to foster long-term partnerships. They focus on supplier performance, contract management, and supplier relationship management to ensure seamless collaboration.

    o Bidding Professional: Bidding professionals build relationships with buyers by delivering high-quality proposals, demonstrating a deep understanding of their needs, and consistently exceeding expectations. They strive to establish themselves as trusted partners who can deliver results.

5. Continuous Improvement:

- o Procurement Professional: Procurement professionals continuously review and optimize procurement processes to enhance efficiency and cost-effectiveness. They monitor supplier performance, identify areas for improvement, and implement strategies to streamline procurement operations.

- o Bidding Professional: Bidding professionals engage in continuous improvement to refine their bidding strategies and enhance their chances of winning contracts. They analyze past performance, gather feedback, and adapt their approach to stay competitive in the ever-evolving bidding landscape.

While procurement professionals focus on sourcing and supplier management, bidding professionals are dedicated to crafting winning proposals and securing contracts.

Procurement professionals are responsible for ensuring that their organization's procurement processes are conducted efficiently, effectively, and in compliance with regulations and policies. Their focus is on evaluating supplier proposals, negotiating contracts, and securing the best value for money. They possess in-depth knowledge of procurement strategies, supplier evaluation, and contract management. Their primary objective is to meet organizational needs while minimizing costs and risks.

On the other hand, bidders and tender management professionals are actively engaged in the process of competing for and winning contracts. Their perspective is shaped by the challenges, strategies, and dynamics specific to the bidding environment. They possess valuable insights into the intricacies of the bidding process, such as crafting winning proposals, conducting competitive analysis, and pricing strategies.

While procurement professionals provide valuable guidance and expertise, their primary concern is not centered around winning contracts. Their focus lies in ensuring a fair and transparent procurement process that delivers the best value for their organization. While they may offer advice to bidding organizations, their perspectives may not fully capture the complexities and nuances involved in tender management.

Learning from active bidders and tender management professionals allows you to tap into their wealth of experience and gain insights into the strategies and tactics that lead to success. These professionals have honed their skills through hands-on involvement in bidding processes, continuous learning, and adaptation to the evolving landscape. They understand the intricacies of developing compelling proposals, identifying competitive advantages, and effectively addressing buyer requirements.

By seeking guidance from bidding professionals who remain actively involved in the field, you benefit from their real-world experiences and the expertise they have developed over time. Their insights into the challenges, pitfalls, and emerging trends in the bidding arena provide a practical and up-to-date perspective that can greatly enhance your bidding strategies.

While procurement professionals bring valuable expertise to the table, their objectives and perspectives differ from those of bidders and tender management professionals. To develop a comprehensive understanding of tender management and increase your chances of winning contracts, it is vital to learn from bidding professionals who have firsthand experience and a proven track record of success. Their insights, strategies, and practical knowledge will equip you with the tools necessary to navigate the competitive bidding landscape successfully.

Potential conflicts can arise between procurement professionals and bidding professionals due to their differing priorities and objectives. These conflicts can have various impacts on the procurement and bidding processes:

1. Conflict of Interest: Procurement professionals are responsible for ensuring fair and unbiased supplier selection, while bidding professionals aim to win contracts for their organization. This inherent conflict

of interest can create tension and challenges in maintaining an objective evaluation process.

2. Limited Collaboration: If procurement professionals and bidding professionals do not collaborate effectively, there may be a lack of communication and understanding between the two parties. This can result in misunderstandings, misaligned expectations, and ultimately, inefficient procurement and bidding processes.

3. Reduced Supplier Innovation: If procurement professionals solely focus on cost reduction and risk mitigation, they may overlook innovative solutions and overlook the value that bidding professionals can bring. This can limit opportunities for suppliers to propose creative and innovative ideas that could benefit the organization.

4. Missed Opportunities: If bidding professionals are not actively engaged with procurement professionals, they may miss out on important information, changes in procurement strategies, or new opportunities. Lack of collaboration can hinder the bidding professionals' ability to tailor their proposals effectively and position themselves as the best-fit supplier.

5. Adversarial Relationships: When conflicts arise between procurement and bidding professionals, it can lead to adversarial relationships, where both parties become more focused on "winning" the negotiation rather than finding mutually beneficial outcomes. This can strain the relationship between the organization and its suppliers, leading to less productive partnerships.

To mitigate these potential conflicts and their impacts, organizations can take proactive steps:

1. Foster Collaboration: Encourage open communication and collaboration between procurement and bidding professionals. Facilitate regular meetings and

knowledge-sharing sessions to ensure alignment and understanding of objectives and strategies.

2. Clearly Define Roles and Expectations: Establish clear roles and responsibilities for procurement and bidding professionals, ensuring that their objectives and success metrics are well-defined. This clarity helps to avoid conflicting priorities and promotes a more cooperative approach.

3. Encourage Cross-Functional Training: Provide opportunities for procurement and bidding professionals to gain insights into each other's roles and perspectives through cross-functional training or job rotations. This enhances their understanding of the broader procurement and bidding processes and promotes empathy and collaboration.

4. Emphasize Mutual Benefit: Promote a culture that recognizes the mutual benefit of successful procurement and bidding outcomes. Encourage a focus on long-term relationships and value creation, rather than adversarial or win-lose scenarios.

5. Continuous Improvement: Encourage ongoing evaluation and improvement of procurement and bidding processes. Involve both procurement and bidding professionals in identifying areas for enhancement and implementing best practices to optimize efficiency and effectiveness.

By addressing potential conflicts and promoting collaboration, organizations can leverage the strengths of both procurement and bidding professionals, leading to more successful procurement outcomes and increased bidding success.

Information Updates

One of the key challenges is discerning which information is truly valuable and applicable to your specific industry and bidding process.

Every industry has its unique dynamics, challenges, and mindsets when it comes to bidding and winning contracts. To ensure you gather relevant and up-to-date information, it is advisable to consult a diverse range of sources. Relying on at least five different sources can provide a broader perspective and a more comprehensive understanding of the best practices and strategies that apply to your specific industry.

It is crucial to be aware that a significant portion of the content available online may be outdated or lack practical relevance. Some resources may focus solely on compliance and technicalities without providing any meaningful insights or strategies to enhance the bidding process or increase the likelihood of a successful bid.

In my view, every tender opportunity and the corresponding tender proposal form a unique microcosm that demands a tailored and creative approach. As a bidder, it is your responsibility to go the extra mile, think outside the box, and do whatever it takes to position yourself for a winning bid. This may involve incorporating innovative solutions, leveraging unique strengths, or proposing value-added initiatives that set you apart from the competition.

To navigate through the sea of information effectively and optimize your bidding strategies, consider the following:

1. Research and Diversify: Invest time in researching and exploring various sources of information, including industry-specific publications, case studies, white papers, and expert insights. Ensure that the information is recent, relevant, and aligns with the specific requirements of your bidding process.

2. Seek Industry Experts: Connect with industry experts, mentors, or consultants who possess extensive experience in successful bidding. Their practical

knowledge and insights can provide invaluable guidance and help you tailor your strategies to maximize your chances of winning contracts.

3.   Network and Collaborate: Engage in networking opportunities within your industry to connect with peers, potential clients, and successful bidders. Share experiences, exchange best practices, and learn from their success stories and challenges. Collaborating with others in the field can expand your knowledge base and open doors to new opportunities.

4.   Continual Learning and Adaptation: Recognize that the bidding landscape is dynamic and continuously evolving. Commit to ongoing learning and professional development to stay updated with industry trends, emerging technologies, and innovative approaches. Be adaptable and willing to modify your strategies based on changing market dynamics and client preferences.

In addition to staying updated with relevant information, it's essential to recognize the potential conflicts and impacts that outdated or irrelevant information can have on your bidding process. Relying on outdated information may lead to inefficiencies, missed opportunities, and ultimately, unsuccessful bids.

Conflicts can arise when outdated information contradicts current industry standards, best practices, or regulatory requirements. This can result in non-compliant bids that are immediately disqualified or fail to meet the expectations of the procurement team. It's crucial to verify the accuracy and currency of the information you encounter to ensure that your bids align with the latest guidelines and expectations.

Moreover, outdated information may fail to capture the evolving needs and preferences of clients and procurement teams. Bid evaluators seek innovative solutions, fresh perspectives, and proposals that address their specific pain points. By relying on outdated information, you may miss out on opportunities to differentiate yourself, showcase your expertise, and align your bid with the client's current priorities.

Another impact of outdated information is the missed opportunity for continuous improvement and growth. The bidding landscape is constantly evolving, and successful bidders adapt their strategies to stay competitive. By relying on outdated approaches, you may overlook emerging trends, technological advancements, or new methodologies that can give you a competitive edge. Embracing up-to-date information allows you to evolve your bidding strategies, incorporate industry best practices, and maximize your chances of success.

To mitigate the risks associated with outdated information, consider the following:

1. Critical Evaluation: Adopt a critical mindset when reviewing information. Assess the credibility of the source, the relevance to your industry and bidding process, and the recency of the information. Scrutinize outdated content and be cautious about applying it directly to your bids.

2. Cross-Referencing: Cross-reference information from multiple reliable sources to validate its accuracy and consistency. Seek corroborating evidence and compare insights to ensure a well-rounded understanding of the subject matter.

3. Continuous Learning: Invest in your professional development by attending industry conferences, workshops, and training programs. Engage in webinars, podcasts, and online forums to stay informed about the latest trends, regulations, and best practices in bidding.

4. Peer Collaboration: Engage with colleagues, peers, and industry networks to exchange knowledge and share experiences. Collaborative discussions can provide valuable insights into current practices,

challenges, and emerging trends, helping you stay updated and refine your bidding strategies.

By remaining vigilant, discerning, and adaptive, you can navigate the abundance of information available, avoid the pitfalls of outdated content, and position yourself for success in the competitive bidding arena. Continual learning, critical evaluation, and staying connected with industry experts will enable you to develop informed and effective bidding strategies that lead to improved bid outcomes and increased contract wins.

Remember, bidding is an intricate process that requires a combination of industry knowledge, strategic thinking, and proactive adaptation. By seeking out reliable and relevant information, continuously improving your skills, and thinking creatively, you can position yourself for success in the competitive world of bidding and contract acquisition.

Resource Disasters

It's crucial to recognize that not all resources are created equal. Different bidding professionals possess varying levels of expertise, experience, and approaches to tender management. Understanding these differences can help you make informed decisions and improve your own bidding process.

Top bidders stand out from the average professionals due to their mindset, approach, and dedication to success. They have accumulated years of experience and consistently win tenders by actively managing the complete tender management process. These professionals go beyond relying solely on their clients' existing information and profiles. They invest in continuous professional development, strategically tackle challenges, and acquire and develop operational business data. They collaborate closely with various stakeholders across their organization, ensuring they have the necessary information to craft excellent proposals. Rather than relying on preexisting content, top bidders take control and reveal hidden strengths to differentiate themselves from the competition.

On the other hand, there are individuals who engage in tender proposals as a secondary responsibility alongside their primary job. Referred to as casual bidders, their focus is more on bid writing rather than the comprehensive tender management cycle and continuous improvement processes. Compliance often takes precedence over innovation, and their approach may be limited to answering the required questions without going beyond the surface. These individuals may rely heavily on existing information and profiles and have limited opportunities for skill improvement and growth.

When seeking advice and information from bidding professionals, it is advisable to diversify your sources. Engaging with a variety of professionals allows you to gain contrasting perspectives and insights. By comparing the approaches of different bidders, you can filter out what works well for your specific scenario and develop a more robust bidding strategy.

For instance, if you consult a casual bidder, they may emphasize the importance of answering questions and focusing on compliance. While this advice holds merit in their context, their primary role and lack of tight deadlines may influence their perspective. In contrast, top bidders would encourage going beyond the questions, providing relevant and impressive content, analyzing feedback for continuous improvement, and working relentlessly to win contracts. Their perspective reflects their experience, drive, and commitment to excellence.

By understanding the nuances and differences among bidding professionals, you can selectively incorporate the best practices and insights that align with your goals and bidding process. Consulting multiple sources allows you to gain a broader understanding of effective strategies and refine your approach accordingly.

Tapping into diverse resources and considering various perspectives is crucial for improving your bidding process. Learning from top bidders who are actively engaged in the game and continuously striving for success can provide valuable insights and inspiration. By gathering information from multiple sources, you can make informed decisions and develop a winning bidding strategy tailored to your specific needs and objectives.

Additionally, understanding the potential biases and limitations of different bidding professionals can help you navigate the complexities of the bidding process more effectively. Casual bidders, while offering valuable insights from their compliance-focused approach, may not possess the same depth of experience and strategic mindset as top bidders. It's important to recognize that their advice may be more applicable to organizations with less demanding bid requirements or those who prioritize meeting minimum compliance standards.

On the other hand, top bidders offer a wealth of knowledge and expertise honed through years of experience and a relentless pursuit of success. They approach each tender with a strategic mindset, going beyond the surface-level requirements to deliver comprehensive and impressive proposals. Their focus on continuous improvement and commitment to understanding the nuances of the bidding process sets them apart. By learning from their perspectives, you can gain valuable insights into how to elevate your bidding strategies, impress evaluators, and increase your chances of securing contracts.

Furthermore, by considering a range of sources and perspectives, you can develop a well-rounded understanding of effective bidding practices. This approach allows you to adapt and tailor strategies to your specific industry, project requirements, and organizational goals. It's important to note that while certain principles and best practices are transferable across industries, each sector may have unique dynamics and nuances that require specialized approaches. Engaging with bidding professionals from diverse sectors can provide you with a broader perspective and expose you to innovative ideas that you can apply within your own industry.

Incorporating a variety of sources and perspectives into your bidding process fosters a culture of continuous learning and improvement. It allows you to stay informed about emerging trends, evolving evaluation criteria, and changing industry dynamics. By actively seeking knowledge and insights from different professionals, you can stay ahead of the competition, refine your strategies, and position your organization as a strong contender in the bidding arena.

Recognizing the differences between casual bidders and top bidders and leveraging the insights from both can greatly enhance your bidding capabilities. By consulting multiple sources, considering various perspectives, and adapting strategies to your specific context, you can develop a comprehensive and effective bidding approach. Embracing a culture of continuous learning and improvement will position you for success in the competitive world of tender management.

Failing to consider multiple perspectives and relying solely on the advice of a single source can lead to disastrous outcomes in the bidding process. Here are some potential disasters that can occur:

1. Limited Perspective: Relying on the advice of only one bidding professional or a single source of information limits your understanding of the complexities and nuances of the bidding process. Each bidding professional brings their unique experiences, strategies, and insights, and by relying on a single perspective, you may overlook critical aspects or miss out on innovative approaches.

2. Ineffective Strategies: Basing your bidding strategies solely on the advice of a casual bidder, who may prioritize compliance over innovation, can hinder your chances of success. While compliance is important, winning bids often require going beyond the basic requirements and delivering proposals that impress evaluators and differentiate your organization from competitors. Failing to recognize this can result in ineffective strategies that fail to capture the attention and interest of the evaluators.

3. Missed Opportunities: By not considering multiple sources, you may miss out on valuable insights and best practices that could significantly improve your bidding process. Top bidders, with their extensive experience and strategic mindset, have developed winning strategies and refined their approaches over time. Ignoring their perspectives means overlooking potential opportunities to enhance your proposals, optimize your business profile, and increase your chances of winning contracts.

4. Stagnation and Lack of Growth: Without exposure to diverse perspectives, you may find yourself stuck in a cycle of mediocrity, repeating the same strategies and failing to evolve. Bidding is a dynamic field, and staying competitive requires continuous learning and improvement. By limiting your information sources, you risk falling behind the industry trends, failing to adapt to changing evaluation criteria, and ultimately hindering your growth and success.

To avoid these disasters, it is crucial to seek insights and perspectives from various bidding professionals, industry experts, and reputable sources. By considering a range of perspectives, you gain a comprehensive understanding of effective bidding practices, innovative strategies, and emerging trends. This enables you to make informed decisions, tailor your approach to specific bid requirements, and maximize your chances of success in the highly competitive bidding landscape.

Staying In Control

The role of a bidder extends beyond simply responding to tender requirements. It requires a proactive and strategic approach to navigate the complexities of the bidding process and secure successful outcomes. One crucial aspect that distinguishes top bidders from the rest is their ability to effectively deal with superiors and address pricing challenges.

Top bidders understand the importance of maintaining control over the bidding process while effectively managing the expectations of their superiors. They take proactive steps to ensure that they have a clear understanding of the project requirements, objectives, and any constraints set by superiors. By staying informed and in control, they can effectively guide the bidding process and make informed decisions.

Staying in control also involves setting realistic expectations with superiors. Top bidders communicate openly and transparently about the potential challenges, risks, and limitations of the bid. They provide accurate timelines, budget estimates, and resource requirements to manage superiors' expectations and avoid any misunderstandings.

Furthermore, top bidders establish clear lines of communication and decision-making authority with superiors. They ensure that they have the necessary autonomy to make timely decisions and take actions that align with the bid strategy and objectives. This allows them to respond promptly to changing circumstances, address any issues that arise, and keep the bid on track.

In situations where superiors may have differing opinions or demands that could potentially jeopardize the success of the bid, top bidders assert their professional expertise and advocate for the best approach. They provide evidence-based arguments, alternative solutions, and recommendations backed by their industry knowledge and experience. By staying in control of the bidding process and guiding superiors towards the most effective course of action, top bidders maximize their chances of achieving success.

Overall, staying in control when dealing with superiors during the bidding process empowers top bidders to effectively lead and navigate the complexities of the bid. It allows them to make informed decisions, set realistic expectations, and advocate for the best interests of the bid and their organization.

Superiors, such as financial directors or decision-makers within the organization, can greatly influence the bidding process, particularly when it comes to pricing. Successful bidders understand the importance of engaging with these superiors and finding ways to align their objectives with the goal of winning contracts. However, this often requires navigating delicate situations and overcoming potential resistance.

When faced with high prices that are deemed noncompetitive, top bidders don't simply accept them as a given. They leverage their industry knowledge and experience to assess the feasibility and profitability of the prices. This critical evaluation allows them to identify potential gaps and explore alternative strategies to increase their chances of success. Rather than shying away from difficult conversations, top bidders take the initiative to engage with superiors and present well-researched data and insights to support their case for more competitive pricing.

One approach utilized by top bidders is to foster a collaborative relationship with superiors, working together to develop pricing strategies that align with the organization's goals and objectives. This involves open and transparent communication, where the bidder showcases the potential benefits of adjusting prices to ensure both the organization and the client can profit from winning contracts. By positioning themselves as strategic partners, top bidders gain the trust and support of superiors, enabling them to make informed decisions and implement necessary adjustments.

However, it is important to note that not all superiors may be open to such discussions or receptive to adjusting pricing. In such cases, top bidders must demonstrate adaptability and resourcefulness to overcome these challenges. They may need to employ alternative strategies, such as seeking competitive pricing data from industry peers, benchmarking against similar projects, or proposing value-added services that can justify the pricing. These innovative approaches showcase the bidder's ability to think outside the box and find creative solutions to achieve a balance between profitability and competitiveness.

The relationship between bidders and superiors is crucial in creating a conducive environment for bidding success. Open lines of communication, mutual trust, and a shared commitment to achieving optimal outcomes are the foundations of this relationship. By actively engaging with superiors, top bidders can leverage their expertise, industry knowledge, and persuasive skills to influence decision-making and ensure that pricing aligns with market expectations and client needs.

Dealing with superiors and addressing pricing challenges are key aspects of the bidding process. Top bidders approach these challenges with confidence, strategic thinking, and effective communication skills. They foster collaborative relationships with superiors, presenting data-driven arguments and proposing innovative solutions to secure more competitive pricing. Their ability to navigate these dynamics sets them apart and increases their chances of achieving repeated bidding success.

Furthermore, the ability to effectively deal with superiors goes beyond addressing pricing challenges. It encompasses building a strong working relationship based on trust, respect, and open communication. Top bidders recognize that superiors play a vital role in shaping the overall bidding strategy and decision-making process.

When engaging with superiors, top bidders go beyond the transactional aspects of bidding and focus on conveying the long-term value and benefits of winning contracts. They emphasize the potential growth opportunities, market expansion, and enhanced brand reputation that can result from successful bids. By highlighting the strategic advantages and alignment with organizational goals, top bidders can garner support and enthusiasm from their superiors.

In some instances, superiors may have concerns or reservations about certain aspects of the bidding process. Rather than dismissing their feedback or opinions, top bidders actively listen and seek to understand their perspectives. This demonstrates a willingness to collaborate and find common ground. They engage in constructive dialogue, addressing any misconceptions or reservations while offering well-informed insights and recommendations to alleviate concerns.

In the face of potential conflicts or disagreements with superiors, top bidders maintain a solution-oriented mindset. They prioritize the best interests of the organization while remaining open to feedback and alternative viewpoints. This approach fosters a sense of teamwork and cooperation, creating an environment where ideas can be freely shared, and decisions can be made collectively.

It's important to note that the relationship between bidders and superiors is a two-way street. Just as top bidders strive to understand the perspectives and objectives of superiors, they also appreciate the importance of effectively communicating their own expertise, experience, and insights. By showcasing their track record of success, industry knowledge, and innovative approaches, top bidders can instill confidence in their superiors and position themselves as trusted advisors in the bidding process.

Ultimately, the ability to navigate the dynamics with superiors is a critical skill for top bidders. It requires a combination of strategic thinking, effective communication, adaptability, and a commitment to achieving mutual success. By fostering strong relationships, actively engaging with superiors, and finding common ground, top bidders can secure the support, resources, and guidance needed to consistently excel in the competitive world of bidding.

n addition to building a strong relationship with superiors, top bidders also understand the importance of effectively managing expectations. They recognize that superiors may have specific goals, priorities, and timelines that need to be considered in the bidding process.

To ensure alignment, top bidders proactively communicate with superiors throughout the bidding journey. They provide regular updates on progress, address any concerns or challenges, and seek input or guidance when necessary. This transparent and proactive approach not only builds trust but also enables superiors to have a clear understanding of the bid's status and any potential risks or opportunities.

Another crucial aspect of managing superiors is the ability to present information in a compelling and persuasive manner. Top bidders are skilled at preparing comprehensive reports, presentations, and proposals that clearly articulate the value proposition, benefits, and competitive advantage of their bid. They use data, metrics, and real-world examples to support their arguments and demonstrate the potential return on investment.

Furthermore, top bidders are adept at adapting their communication style and content to suit the preferences of their superiors. They take the time to understand the decision-making process, preferred formats, and key factors that influence their superiors' choices. By tailoring their messages to resonate with superiors' needs and expectations, top bidders can increase their chances of securing support and approval for their bids.

In instances where superiors may have conflicting opinions or demands, top bidders skillfully navigate through these challenges. They remain focused on the overarching goal of winning contracts while finding creative solutions or compromises that satisfy the concerns of all stakeholders. This requires strong negotiation and problem-solving skills, as well as the ability to balance multiple perspectives and priorities.

Ultimately, the success of a bidder is often intertwined with their ability to effectively engage and manage superiors. By building strong relationships, managing expectations, and presenting compelling information, top bidders can position themselves as trusted advisors and secure the necessary support and resources to consistently achieve bidding success.

Design Relevance

A well-designed tender proposal goes beyond just visual appeal. It serves as a powerful tool to effectively communicate key messages, highlight strengths, and differentiate the bidder from competitors. By incorporating design principles, the bidder can create a cohesive and engaging document that captures the attention of the procurement team and leaves a lasting impression.

One aspect where design can have a significant impact is in the organization and structure of the proposal. A clear and intuitive layout, with well-defined sections and headings, allows the evaluators to easily navigate through the document and locate the information they need. Effective use of headings, subheadings, and bullet points helps to break down complex information into digestible chunks, enhancing readability and comprehension.

Visual elements such as graphs, charts, and diagrams can also play a crucial role in presenting data and supporting arguments. They provide a visual representation of information, making it easier for evaluators to understand complex concepts or statistical data. Well-designed visuals not only enhance the clarity of information but also make the proposal more visually appealing and memorable.

Incorporating branding elements and consistent design elements throughout the proposal helps to reinforce the bidder's identity and create a professional and cohesive visual presence. Consistent use of colors, fonts, and graphics in alignment with the bidder's branding guidelines can create a sense of brand recognition and familiarity.

Attention to detail is another important aspect of design. A well-designed proposal shows professionalism and meticulousness, reflecting the bidder's commitment to quality. Paying attention to elements such as proper formatting, alignment, and spacing can enhance the overall visual impression and create a polished and professional look.

While design can enhance the overall presentation of a tender proposal, it is essential to remember that content remains the primary focus. The design should serve to support and enhance the content, not overshadow or compensate for weak or insufficient information. A visually appealing design will only be effective if it is backed by well-crafted content that addresses the buyer's needs, provides evidence of capabilities, and presents a compelling solution.

A well-designed tender proposal, when combined with strong content, can make a lasting impact on the procurement team. By considering layout, visual elements, branding, and attention to detail, bidders can create a visually appealing and compelling document that effectively communicates their expertise and value proposition. It is the synergy between design and content that creates a winning bid, capturing the attention and confidence of the evaluators.

The design of a tender proposal can also influence the perception of professionalism and attention to detail. A visually appealing and well-designed document conveys a sense of credibility and competence, instilling confidence in the procurement team. On the other hand, a poorly designed proposal with inconsistent formatting, cluttered layout, or unclear visuals may give the impression of a lack of professionalism and may undermine the bidder's credibility.

Moreover, design elements can be strategically utilized to emphasize key points and highlight the bidder's unique selling proposition. The use of visual hierarchy, such as bold headings, subheadings, and bullet points, can draw attention to important information and make it easier for evaluators to grasp the key messages. Thoughtful use of colors, fonts, and graphics can evoke specific emotions or associations that align with the bidder's brand identity and value proposition.

Design also plays a role in creating a memorable and engaging tender proposal. Human beings are naturally drawn to aesthetically pleasing visuals, and a well-designed document has the potential to capture and retain the attention of the evaluators. This can be especially advantageous in a competitive bidding environment, where evaluators are reviewing numerous proposals. A visually appealing design can make the bidder's proposal stand out from the rest and leave a positive and lasting impression.

It is worth noting that design considerations should align with the expectations and preferences of the procurement team. Different organizations may have different aesthetic preferences or formatting requirements. It is crucial to carefully review the tender documentation and any guidelines provided by the buyer to ensure compliance with their design expectations.

While design can enhance the overall impression of a tender proposal, it should not overshadow or compensate for weak content. The content of the proposal should always take precedence, providing comprehensive and compelling information that addresses the buyer's needs and demonstrates the bidder's capabilities. The design should serve as a complement to the content, enhancing its presentation and impact.

The design of a tender proposal can have a significant influence on the perception and effectiveness of the bid. A well-designed document conveys professionalism, highlights key points, engages the evaluators, and creates a positive impression. By striking a balance between design and content, bidders can create visually appealing and impactful proposals that increase their chances of success in the competitive bidding process.

While design plays a role in creating a visually appealing and engaging tender proposal, the content remains the most critical factor in determining its impact. Content carries the substantive information and persuasive arguments that directly address the buyer's requirements and demonstrate the bidder's qualifications and capabilities. Here are a few reasons why content is more impactful than design:

1. Substance over style: At its core, the tender evaluation process focuses on evaluating the bidder's ability to meet the buyer's needs and deliver value. The content of the proposal provides the necessary

information to demonstrate how the bidder intends to fulfill those requirements. The clarity, specificity, and relevance of the content carry more weight in determining the proposal's effectiveness than its visual design.

2. Clear communication: The content of a tender proposal conveys the bidder's understanding of the buyer's needs, their proposed solution, and the value they offer. A well-crafted and comprehensive response that effectively communicates these aspects is more likely to resonate with the evaluators and address their concerns. Clear and concise language, supported by evidence and examples, allows the buyer to assess the bidder's capabilities accurately.

3. Substantive evidence: Bidders must provide compelling evidence of their experience, expertise, and past performance to establish credibility and demonstrate their ability to deliver successful outcomes. This evidence is typically presented through case studies, references, qualifications, and other supporting documents. The quality and relevance of the evidence carry far more weight in decision-making than the visual design elements of the proposal.

4. Compliance with buyer requirements: The content of a tender proposal must adhere to the buyer's guidelines, specifications, and evaluation criteria. Failure to comply with these requirements can result in disqualification or a significant reduction in scores, regardless of the design quality. Evaluators focus primarily on assessing whether the proposal meets the buyer's specific requirements, rather than being swayed by the aesthetics of the design.

5. Evaluation criteria emphasis: The evaluation criteria set by the buyer typically prioritize factors such as technical capability, experience, pricing, and compliance. These criteria directly align with the content of the proposal rather than its design.

Evaluators assign scores based on how well the bidder addresses these criteria, and the content provides the primary basis for evaluation.

Design can still enhance the visual appeal, readability, and organization of a tender proposal, it should serve as a complement to the content rather than overshadowing it. A well-designed proposal can create a positive impression and engage the evaluators, but it is ultimately the substantive content that conveys the bidder's capabilities, value proposition, and alignment with the buyer's requirements. Strong content that addresses the buyer's needs and presents a compelling case for selection is the key to a truly impactful tender proposal.

Size Conflicts

The biggest problem with size limitations in tender responses is the potential compromise of content quality and relevance. When bidders are restricted by word counts or page limits, there is a risk of sacrificing important information, clarity, and coherence in an attempt to fit everything within the given space. This can result in a disjointed and ineffective response that fails to address the buyer's needs or effectively showcase the bidder's capabilities.

The pressure to meet size constraints may lead bidders to prioritize quantity over quality, resorting to including excessive and irrelevant information just to fill the available space. This approach not only dilutes the impact of the response but also makes it harder for evaluators to find the relevant details and assess the bidder's suitability for the project. It may also create a perception of disorganization and lack of attention to detail.

Another challenge is the potential loss of key differentiators and value propositions. Bidders may struggle to effectively communicate their unique selling points and competitive advantages within the limited space, thereby missing opportunities to stand out from other bidders. Without clear differentiation, the response may appear generic and fail to capture the attention and interest of the procurement team.

Furthermore, size limitations can hinder the bidder's ability to provide comprehensive evidence, case studies, or detailed explanations that support their claims and demonstrate their capabilities. Evaluators may find it difficult to evaluate the bidder's expertise and experience if the response lacks sufficient supporting documentation or substantiation.

Overall, the biggest problem with size limitations is the potential compromise of content quality, relevance, and the bidder's ability to effectively convey their strengths and differentiate themselves. It requires careful planning, concise writing, and strategic selection of information to ensure that the response remains focused, impactful, and persuasive within the given constraints.

Procurement teams often impose word or page limits on tender responses to streamline the evaluation process and manage their workload effectively. These limitations are designed to ensure fairness and standardize the evaluation criteria for all bidders. As a bidder, it is crucial to understand the importance of following these limits while still maximizing the impact of your content within the given constraints.

While it may seem challenging to convey a comprehensive message within restricted word or page counts, there are strategies you can employ to make the most of the available space. One effective approach is to leverage visual elements and data representation techniques. Graphs, charts, and tables can condense complex information into a concise and easily understandable format, allowing you to convey key points effectively. By presenting data visually, you can communicate a wealth of information in a highly efficient manner. However, it's important to verify with the procurement team how they evaluate and interpret visual content to ensure it aligns with their expectations.

When faced with limitations such as two A4 pages, careful consideration of formatting and layout can help optimize content density. Narrowing margins, using single lines instead of double spacing, and eliminating unnecessary spaces between paragraphs can allow you to fit more relevant information onto each page. However, it is crucial to strike a balance between maximizing content and maintaining readability. Overly dense or cluttered formatting can hinder the evaluators' ability to absorb and comprehend your message. Always review the procurement team's instructions and formatting guidelines to ensure compliance with their requirements.

While the temptation to provide additional content may arise, it is crucial to prioritize relevance and clarity. Evaluators seek concise and focused responses that directly address the buyer's needs and requirements. Adding excessive or tangential information that does not directly align with the question at hand can dilute the impact of your response and create confusion for the evaluators. Quality trumps quantity. Each piece of information should serve a specific purpose, contributing meaningfully to showcase your capabilities and address the buyer's concerns.

Ultimately, the key to success within the limitations of word or page counts is a thoughtful and strategic approach. Prioritize clarity, relevance, and compliance with the procurement team's guidelines. By optimizing the use of space, leveraging visual elements effectively, and delivering concise and impactful content, you can create a tender response that stands out and maximizes your chances of success.

In addition to focusing on content relevance and efficient use of space, it's important to recognize that adherence to the procurement team's instructions is crucial. Failure to comply with their guidelines can result in disqualification or a negative evaluation. Therefore, it is essential to carefully review the instructions provided by the procurement team and ensure that your response aligns with their requirements.

Moreover, when faced with size limitations, it is essential to prioritize the quality and clarity of your content over simply adding more information. Bidders sometimes make the mistake of trying to include as much information as possible within the given constraints, often resulting in a cluttered and unfocused response. Instead, focus on providing concise, well-structured, and impactful content that directly addresses the buyer's needs and showcases your unique value proposition.

Another aspect to consider is the evaluation process itself. Procurement teams typically employ a scoring system or evaluation criteria to assess tender responses. Understanding these criteria is vital for tailoring your content to meet the evaluators' expectations. By aligning your response with the specified criteria, you increase the likelihood of receiving a favorable evaluation.

Furthermore, it is important to remember that size limitations should not hinder your ability to effectively communicate your strengths and differentiate yourself from competitors. Highlighting key differentiators, such as unique expertise, proven track record, or innovative approaches, can help create a memorable impression and increase your chances of success.

Lastly, continuous improvement and learning from past experiences play a crucial role in optimizing your tender responses. Take the time to analyze feedback and evaluation results from previous bids to identify areas for improvement. This allows you to refine your content strategy, strengthen weaknesses, and capitalize on strengths for future opportunities.

Here are 12 common challenges associated with size limitations in tender responses, along with potential solutions:

1. Limited Word/Page Count: One of the primary challenges is the restricted space available to present a comprehensive and compelling response. Bidders must carefully select and prioritize the most critical information to include.

2. Conveying Value: It can be challenging to convey the value of your proposal within the limited space. Focus on succinctly articulating your unique value proposition, emphasizing the benefits and outcomes you can deliver.

3. Complying with Instructions: Following the instructions provided by the procurement team is crucial. Bidders must ensure that their responses adhere to the specified word or page limits while still conveying their key messages effectively.

4. Contextualizing Content: Providing sufficient context and background information can be difficult when space is limited. Bidders should aim to strike a balance between providing essential context and directly addressing the tender requirements.

5. Highlighting Experience: Demonstrating relevant experience and expertise can be challenging within the size constraints. Prioritize showcasing your most significant and impactful projects that align closely with the tender requirements.

6. Addressing Evaluation Criteria: Bidders must address the evaluation criteria effectively, even within limited space. Clearly structure your response to address each criterion explicitly, providing concise and focused evidence of your capabilities.

7. Conveying Technical Details: Presenting technical details or specifications can be challenging in a condensed format. Use tables, diagrams, or bullet points to convey technical information efficiently and clearly.

8. Demonstrating Innovation: It can be difficult to showcase innovative ideas or solutions within limited space. Focus on highlighting key innovative features or approaches that differentiate your proposal from competitors.

9. Managing Supporting Documentation: Bidders often struggle with including supporting documentation, such as case studies or testimonials, within the given limitations. Consider referencing these documents in your response and provide access to them upon request.

10. Avoiding Repetition: Space limitations require bidders to avoid repetition and ensure that each word contributes meaningfully. Review your response carefully to eliminate redundant information and streamline your argument.

11. Visual Presentation: Incorporating visual elements, such as charts or graphics, can be challenging within restricted space. Use visuals strategically to enhance clarity and impact, but ensure they are relevant and contribute to the overall message.

12. Editing and Proofreading: With limited space, it's crucial to thoroughly edit and proofread your response. Remove any unnecessary words or phrases, clarify language, and ensure the response is error-free and polished.

These challenges can be addressed through careful planning, concise writing, effective organization, and strategic use of visuals and supporting documentation. By considering these challenges and implementing appropriate strategies, bidders can optimize their tender responses and increase their chances of success.

Size limitations in tender responses may pose challenges, so, approaching them strategically and prioritizing quality content over quantity can help you make the most of the available space. By carefully adhering to the procurement team's instructions, delivering concise and relevant content, understanding evaluation criteria, and continuously improving your approach, you can optimize your tender responses and increase your chances of success in the competitive bidding process.

Impactful Structure

he structure of a tender proposal or response plays a critical role in effectively conveying information and maximizing the chances of success. Here are some key points to consider when it comes to the impact of structure:

1. Clarity and Time-Saving: A well-structured response helps the procurement team save time by presenting information in a clear and organized manner. It enables them to quickly navigate through the content and locate the relevant details they need to evaluate.

2. Relevance and Connection: The structure should facilitate a strong connection between the content and the specific questions and requirements of the tender. Each section or subsection should directly address the key points raised, ensuring that the response remains focused and on-topic.

3. Providing Evidence: An effective structure allows for the seamless integration of supporting evidence within the response. Whether it's case studies, references, or testimonials, the structure should provide clear indications of where and how this evidence supports the claims and demonstrates the bidder's capabilities.

4. Easy Understanding: The structure should promote readability and comprehension. It involves breaking down the response into logical sections, using headings, subheadings, bullet points, and numbering to guide the reader's attention. This approach helps to make the content more digestible and allows the procurement team to grasp the main points effortlessly.

5. Clear Explanation of Relevance: The structure should enable the bidder to explain why the presented content is relevant to the tender and how it addresses the specific requirements. Clear connections and explanations help the procurement team understand the bidder's thought process and rationale.

6. Effective Use of Formatting: When dealing with extensive content, the structure can be enhanced through the strategic use of formatting elements such as colors, fonts, paragraphs, and sub-titles. These visual cues can help differentiate sections, highlight key information, and improve overall readability.

7. Summarizing Key Elements: If space permits, it is beneficial to include summary sections that highlight the key elements of the response and link them explicitly to the tender requirements. This approach allows the procurement team to quickly grasp the bidder's strengths and value proposition.

8. Avoiding Information Overload: While it's important to provide sufficient information, overloading the response with excessive content can hinder readability and comprehension. If the structure becomes overly complex or convoluted, it may be wise to prioritize concise and focused content instead.

9. Maintaining Logical Flow: A well-structured response maintains a logical flow of information, allowing the procurement team to follow the bidder's argument or narrative smoothly. Each section should build upon the previous one and lead naturally into the next, creating a cohesive and coherent presentation of ideas.

10. Emphasizing Key Points: Structure can be used to emphasize the most critical points or unique selling propositions of the bidder. By strategically placing these key points within the response, such as in headings or bullet points, they are more likely to capture the attention of the procurement team and leave a lasting impression.

11. Supporting Readability and Skim-ability: A clear structure aids in readability and skim-ability, enabling the procurement team to quickly assess the content. Subheadings and bullet points help break down information into digestible chunks, making it easier for

evaluators to scan and locate specific details of interest.

12. Adhering to Evaluation Criteria: A well-structured response aligns with the evaluation criteria set by the procurement team. By organizing the content according to the specified evaluation factors, the bidder demonstrates their understanding of the evaluation process and ensures that their response is evaluated effectively and fairly.

The biggest problem that can arise from a poor or inadequate structure is the risk of the procurement team misunderstanding or missing crucial information. If the response is disorganized, lacks clarity, or fails to effectively connect the content to the tender requirements, the evaluators may struggle to comprehend the bidder's strengths and value proposition. This can result in a lower score or even disqualification if the response is deemed incomprehensible or irrelevant.

If you encounter a poorly structured response, a quick fix is to review and reorganize the content to create a more logical and reader-friendly structure. Start by identifying the main points and organizing them into clear sections or headings. Use bullet points, numbering, or visual elements to highlight key information and make it more accessible. Ensure that there is a logical flow between sections and that each paragraph or sentence contributes to the overall coherence of the response. By investing some time and effort into restructuring the content, you can significantly improve the clarity and impact of your bid.

Mastering the skill of structuring content is crucial for bidders to effectively convey their message, highlight their strengths, and ensure their responses are easy to navigate and understand. By carefully organizing and presenting information, bidders can make a strong impression on the procurement team and increase their chances of success.

On Writing

The writing style and skill employed in a tender proposal play a crucial role in effectively conveying information, engaging the reader, and influencing the evaluation process. While it may not be the sole factor that determines the success of a bid, it significantly impacts how the proposal is perceived and evaluated by the procurement team.

Tender proposal writing is a complex and dynamic process that requires a deep understanding of the buyer's requirements, effective communication skills, and strategic thinking. By exploring various strategies and best practices, bidders can optimize their approach and increase their chances of success.

One area to explore is the use of technology and digital tools to streamline the tender proposal writing process. Online collaboration platforms, document management systems, and project management software can enhance team collaboration, improve document organization, and ensure timely submission of proposals. Exploring and leveraging these tools can save time, improve efficiency, and enhance the overall quality of the proposal.

Another aspect to explore is the power of data and analytics. Bidders can harness the power of data to gain insights into market trends, competitor analysis, and buyer preferences. By conducting thorough research and analysis, bidders can align their proposal with the buyer's needs, identify unique selling points, and present data-driven arguments that strengthen their case. Exploring data-driven approaches can provide a competitive edge and demonstrate a commitment to evidence-based decision-making.

Furthermore, bidders can explore the benefits of storytelling and narrative techniques in their tender proposals. Crafting a compelling narrative that resonates with the buyer can evoke emotions, capture attention, and make the proposal memorable. By weaving a story that showcases the bidder's expertise, experience, and value proposition, bidders can create a persuasive and engaging proposal that stands out from the competition.

In addition, exploring effective communication strategies can significantly impact the clarity and coherence of a tender proposal. Bidders should consider the use of plain language, concise writing, and visual aids to present complex information in an accessible manner. By using clear and concise language, bidders can ensure that the evaluators can easily understand and assess the proposal. Exploring different communication techniques, such as infographics, charts, and diagrams, can further enhance the visual appeal and comprehension of the proposal.

Moreover, bidders can explore the concept of continuous improvement in their tender proposal writing process. This involves learning from past experiences, seeking feedback from evaluators, and consistently refining and optimizing the proposal. By embracing a growth mindset and actively seeking opportunities to improve, bidders can enhance their skills, adapt to changing requirements, and increase their chances of winning future contracts.

Bidders should consider involving relevant stakeholders, such as subject matter experts, project managers, and sales teams, throughout the proposal development process. By leveraging the collective knowledge and expertise of the team, bidders can enhance the quality and accuracy of the proposal, address potential gaps, and ensure a comprehensive and well-rounded submission.

By exploring various strategies, tools, and approaches, bidders can continuously enhance their tender proposal writing skills. The exploration of new techniques, technologies, and methodologies can lead to innovation, improved competitiveness, and higher success rates. Bidders who are open to exploration and embrace a growth mindset are better positioned to adapt to evolving market dynamics and deliver compelling and winning tender proposals.

Clear and coherent writing is essential for ensuring that the content of the proposal is understood and appreciated by the evaluators. A well-crafted writing style not only enhances readability but also instills confidence in the bidder's professionalism, attention to detail, and ability to deliver on the contract.

Numerous studies have examined the correlation between writing quality and bid success, consistently showing that well-written proposals tend to receive higher scores and have a greater chance of winning contracts. These studies emphasize the importance of effective communication through clear, concise, and persuasive writing.

We found that proposals with strong writing skills, including proper grammar, sentence structure, and organization, were perceived as more professional and credible. In contrast, proposals with errors, inconsistencies, and convoluted language were seen as less polished and trustworthy, potentially undermining the bidder's chances of success.

Moreover, writing style can influence the evaluators' perception of the bidder's attention to detail, ability to follow instructions, and overall commitment to quality. A proposal that demonstrates meticulous writing, free from grammatical and spelling errors, conveys a sense of professionalism and dedication to delivering high-quality work. In contrast, a poorly written proposal with numerous mistakes can raise doubts about the bidder's competence and reliability.

Challenges in writing style that can negatively impact a tender proposal are diverse and include:

1. Grammar and Spelling Errors: Mistakes in grammar, punctuation, and spelling can undermine the credibility of the bidder and create doubts about their attention to detail and professionalism. Such errors can distract the evaluators from the content and weaken the overall impact of the proposal.

2. Complex and Confusing Language: Proposals filled with convoluted sentences, technical jargon, and excessive use of industry-specific terms can hinder comprehension and diminish the persuasiveness of the bid. Clear and concise language is essential for effectively conveying ideas and ensuring that the

proposal is accessible to evaluators from various backgrounds.

3. Lack of Coherence and Flow: Incoherent writing, disjointed paragraphs, and a lack of logical structure can make it difficult for evaluators to follow the flow of the proposal. A well-organized and cohesive structure, with clear transitions between ideas, helps maintain the reader's engagement and facilitates a better understanding of the bidder's message.

4. Ineffective Use of Language: Overuse of generic phrases, buzzwords, and clichés can dilute the impact of the proposal and make it sound generic or insincere. Bidders should strive for authenticity and originality in their writing, presenting their unique value proposition and differentiating themselves from competitors.

To address these challenges and improve writing style in tender proposals, bidders can employ several strategies:

1. Proofreading and Editing: Thoroughly review the proposal to identify and correct any grammar, spelling, or punctuation errors. Utilize grammar-checking tools or enlist the help of a professional editor to ensure accuracy and coherence.

2. Clarity and Simplicity: Strive for clear and concise language, avoiding excessive complexity or unnecessary technical terms. Break down complex ideas into digestible chunks and use plain language to ensure the evaluators can easily grasp the bidder's message.

3. Logical Organization: Structure the proposal in a logical and coherent manner, using headings, subheadings, and bullet points to guide the evaluators through the content. Present information in a way that is easy to navigate and locate specific details.

4. Tone and Voice: Maintain a professional and confident tone throughout the proposal, adapting the

language to the target audience while staying true to the bidder's brand voice. Avoid overly formal or informal language and strive for a balance that inspires confidence and trust.

5.   Seek Feedback: Engage colleagues, subject matter experts, or trusted individuals to provide feedback on the writing style, clarity, and persuasiveness of the proposal. Incorporate their suggestions to enhance the overall quality of the writing.

Writing a compelling tender proposal requires a combination of strategic thinking, effective communication, and meticulous attention to detail. It is an essential skill for businesses aiming to secure contracts and win new opportunities. By honing your tender proposal writing skills, you can maximize your chances of success in the competitive bidding process.

1.   Understand the Requirements: Before diving into writing the proposal, thoroughly analyze the tender documents to gain a clear understanding of the buyer's requirements, evaluation criteria, and desired outcomes. This will help you tailor your response to address their specific needs and demonstrate your alignment with their objectives.

2.   Plan and Structure: Develop a comprehensive plan that outlines the key sections and content you need to include in your proposal. Create a logical structure that flows smoothly, guiding the reader through your response and highlighting the most important information. Consider using headings, subheadings, and bullet points to enhance readability and navigation.

3.   Craft a Compelling Introduction: Start your proposal with a captivating introduction that grabs the reader's attention and clearly articulates your understanding of the project and your unique value proposition. Clearly state how your solution addresses the buyer's challenges and delivers tangible benefits.

4. Focus on Clear and Concise Language: Use clear, concise, and jargon-free language to ensure that your proposal is easily understood by the evaluators. Avoid unnecessary technical terms or complex explanations that may confuse or alienate the reader. Communicate your ideas in a straightforward manner to enhance clarity and impact.

5. Provide Evidence and Examples: Back up your claims with solid evidence and relevant examples. Incorporate case studies, previous project successes, client testimonials, and key performance indicators to demonstrate your track record of delivering high-quality results. This substantiates your credibility and strengthens your proposal's persuasiveness.

6. Showcase Your Differentiators: Highlight what sets you apart from your competitors. Clearly articulate your unique selling points, competitive advantages, and innovative approaches that make your solution the best choice. Emphasize how your expertise, resources, and capabilities align with the buyer's needs and position you as the ideal partner.

7. Pay Attention to Formatting and Design: Present your proposal in a visually appealing and professional format. Use consistent fonts, appropriate headings, and a well-organized layout to enhance readability. Incorporate visual elements such as graphs, charts, and infographics to illustrate complex data and make it more digestible for the reader.

8. Review, Revise, and Proofread: Take the time to review and revise your proposal multiple times to ensure clarity, coherence, and accuracy. Pay attention to grammar, spelling, and punctuation errors, as they can undermine your professionalism and credibility. Seek feedback from colleagues or trusted individuals to gain valuable insights and perspectives.

9. Tailor Your Proposal: Customize your proposal to address the specific requirements and priorities of

each tender. Avoid using generic, boilerplate content that fails to directly address the buyer's needs. Tailoring your proposal shows your commitment and dedication to meeting the buyer's expectations.

10. Continuous Improvement: Learn from each tender proposal experience and incorporate feedback into your future submissions. Identify areas for improvement, refine your writing style, and stay updated on industry trends and best practices. Embrace a mindset of continuous improvement to consistently enhance the quality and effectiveness of your tender proposals.

11. Collaborate with Subject Matter Experts: Engage with subject matter experts within your organization to gather insights and expertise relevant to the tender proposal. Collaborate with them to ensure accurate and comprehensive information is included in your response. Their input can enhance the technical aspects of your proposal and lend credibility to your claims.

12. Align with the Evaluation Criteria: Familiarize yourself with the evaluation criteria outlined in the tender documents. Structure your proposal in a way that directly addresses each criterion, providing clear and specific responses. This demonstrates your ability to meet the buyer's requirements and increases your chances of scoring well during the evaluation process.

13. Use Persuasive Language: Craft your proposal using persuasive language that appeals to the emotions and logic of the evaluators. Clearly communicate the benefits and outcomes of choosing your solution, emphasizing the value it brings to the buyer. Use persuasive techniques such as storytelling, compelling statistics, and persuasive arguments to influence the evaluators' decision-making process.

14. Maintain a Professional Tone: Maintain a professional and respectful tone throughout your proposal. Avoid

overly aggressive or confrontational language that may alienate the evaluators. Present your ideas and arguments in a confident and assertive manner while remaining courteous and diplomatic.

15. Follow Guidelines and Submission Requirements: Adhere to all the guidelines and submission requirements outlined in the tender documents. Failure to comply with these instructions can result in disqualification. Pay attention to formatting, page limits, and any specific document formats requested by the buyer.

16. Seek Feedback: If you have the opportunity, request feedback on your tender proposal, especially in cases where you did not win the contract. Feedback can provide valuable insights into areas of improvement, allowing you to refine your approach and enhance future proposals.

17. Stay Updated on Industry Trends: Continuously educate yourself on industry trends, emerging technologies, and best practices related to the products or services you offer. Incorporate this knowledge into your tender proposals to demonstrate your awareness of the latest developments and your ability to deliver innovative solutions.

18. Emphasize Risk Mitigation: Address the buyer's concerns regarding risk by highlighting your risk mitigation strategies. Show that you have considered potential challenges and have proactive measures in place to minimize risks and ensure successful project implementation. This instills confidence in the buyer and positions you as a reliable partner.

19. Demonstrate Flexibility: Showcase your willingness to collaborate and adapt to the buyer's changing needs. Highlight your ability to customize your solution, provide alternative options, and accommodate any modifications required throughout the contract period.

This flexibility demonstrates your commitment to meeting the buyer's evolving requirements.

20. Maintain Ethical Standards: Uphold the highest ethical standards in your tender proposal writing. Avoid misrepresenting information, making false claims, or engaging in unethical practices. Maintaining integrity and transparency in your proposal builds trust with the buyer and enhances your reputation as a reliable and ethical business partner.

By following these best practices and investing in the development of your tender proposal writing skills, you can position yourself as a top bidder who consistently delivers compelling, well-crafted proposals that stand out from the competition and secure coveted contracts.

By improving writing style and skill in tender proposals, bidders can elevate the impact of their content, enhance readability, and increase their chances of success. A well-crafted and engaging writing style demonstrates professionalism, attention to detail, and the ability to communicate effectively, setting the bidder apart from the competition and leaving a positive impression on the evaluators.

Relationships

Creating strong links between your organization and the requirements of the contract is a crucial aspect of developing a compelling tender proposal. By presenting information about your organization in a humble tone and highlighting the perspectives of your clients, you can establish credibility and showcase why your organization is the right choice.

When discussing your clients, it's important to go beyond mere name-dropping. Instead, focus on demonstrating why your clients preferred your organization and what specific aspects they liked about your services. This could include highlighting successful projects, exceptional customer service, or innovative solutions that have positively impacted your clients' businesses. By sharing these client experiences, you create a narrative that connects your organization's capabilities to the needs of the buyer.

In addition, showcasing the achievements and qualifications of your staff members can further strengthen the link between your organization and the contract requirements. Highlight any relevant certifications, industry recognition, or specialized expertise that your team possesses. By demonstrating the expertise and qualifications of your staff, you establish trust and credibility, showing that your organization has the necessary skills to deliver on the contract's objectives.

To effectively link this information to the contract requirements, it is crucial to clearly articulate how these achievements and client experiences directly align with the specific needs outlined in the tender. Clearly outline how your organization's track record, expertise, and client satisfaction directly relate to the buyer's desired outcomes. By making these connections explicit, you demonstrate your understanding of the contract requirements and show how your organization is uniquely positioned to deliver value.

Furthermore, it is essential to avoid excessive self-promotion and instead focus on providing objective evidence of your organization's capabilities. Rather than making bold claims without substantiation, back up your statements with concrete examples, data, and testimonials. This helps the evaluators to see the real impact and value your organization can bring to the contract.

When developing your tender proposal, make it a priority to create strong links between your organization and the requirements of the contract. Present your organization's information in a humble tone, highlighting client perspectives and staff achievements. By effectively linking this information to the contract requirements, you establish credibility, demonstrate understanding, and increase your chances of success. Remember, the key is to provide relevant and compelling evidence that clearly shows how your organization can meet and exceed the buyer's expectations.

Additionally, it is important to go beyond surface-level connections and delve deeper into the specific needs and objectives of the buyer. This requires a thorough understanding of the contract requirements and an ability to identify how your organization can address those needs effectively.

To create strong links, conduct a comprehensive analysis of the buyer's requirements and identify key points where your organization's strengths align with their needs. Highlight these points in your proposal and emphasize how your organization can provide unique solutions or value-added services that directly address the buyer's challenges.

For example, if the contract requires expertise in sustainability practices, showcase your organization's commitment to environmentally-friendly initiatives and highlight specific projects or certifications that demonstrate your expertise in this area. By making these connections explicit, you show the buyer that you have a deep understanding of their priorities and are well-positioned to deliver results.

Furthermore, consider the broader context of the industry and market trends when creating links between your organization and the contract requirements. Stay informed about the latest advancements, technologies, and best practices relevant to the buyer's industry. This enables you to offer innovative solutions and position your organization as a forward-thinking partner.

Support your claims with evidence and data to strengthen the links you create. Include case studies, success stories, and testimonials that showcase your organization's past performance and ability to deliver results. Quantifiable metrics such as cost savings, efficiency improvements, or customer satisfaction ratings provide concrete evidence of your capabilities.

Lastly, ensure that your writing style is clear, concise, and tailored to the needs of the reader. Use plain language and avoid jargon or technical terms that may confuse or alienate the evaluators. A well-structured and coherent proposal that effectively communicates your organization's strengths and how they align with the contract requirements will leave a lasting impression on the procurement team.

Creating strong links between your organization and the contract requirements is crucial for a compelling tender proposal. By understanding the buyer's needs, highlighting relevant expertise, demonstrating innovation, and providing concrete evidence of your past performance, you can establish credibility and increase your chances of success. Remember to approach the proposal from the perspective of the buyer, showcasing how your organization can provide the best solutions and deliver value.

In addition to creating links between your organization and the contract requirements, it is essential to focus on the benefits and outcomes that your organization can deliver. Buyers are not just looking for a list of features or qualifications; they want to understand how choosing your organization will positively impact their project or business.

When crafting your proposal, emphasize the value proposition that sets your organization apart from competitors. Clearly articulate the unique benefits and advantages that your organization brings to the table. This could include factors such as cost-effectiveness, efficiency gains, quality assurance, scalability, or customized solutions tailored to the buyer's specific needs.

To strengthen the link between your organization and the desired outcomes, provide concrete examples and success stories. Showcase how your organization has successfully tackled similar challenges or projects in the past, highlighting measurable results and the satisfaction of previous clients. This evidence helps to build trust and confidence in your organization's ability to deliver on its promises.

Furthermore, consider incorporating a strong focus on the long-term relationship and partnership with the buyer. Highlight your organization's commitment to ongoing support, collaboration, and continuous improvement. Demonstrate how you will not only meet the immediate needs of the contract but also strive to exceed expectations and contribute to the buyer's long-term success.

To enhance the impact of your proposal, leverage relevant industry research and insights. Stay informed about market trends, emerging technologies, and regulatory changes that could impact the buyer's industry. By demonstrating your knowledge and expertise in these areas, you position your organization as a strategic partner who can provide valuable guidance and adapt to evolving needs.

Lastly, ensure that your proposal is well-structured, logically organized, and easy to navigate. Use headings, subheadings, and bullet points to break down complex information into digestible chunks. This makes it easier for evaluators to find key information and assess the alignment between your organization and the contract requirements.

Creating strong links between your organization and the desired outcomes of the buyer is crucial for a compelling tender proposal. By emphasizing the unique benefits, showcasing success stories, focusing on long-term partnership, leveraging industry insights, and presenting information in a clear and organized manner, you can position your organization as the ideal choice. Remember, the goal is to convince the buyer that selecting your organization will lead to the best possible outcomes and deliver significant value.

Differentiating Pitch Values

In the world of bidding and sales, understanding the differences between features, advantages, and benefits is essential for creating persuasive proposals and winning contracts. It is a common mistake to overlook the opportunity to effectively communicate these elements and their connection to the contract requirements and buyer's needs.

Features refer to the distinctive characteristics or qualities of a product, service, or solution. They are the tangible attributes that set your offering apart from others. Examples of features could include advanced technology, specific functionalities, or unique design elements. While features are important to highlight, they alone do not fully capture the value proposition.

Advantages, on the other hand, are the specific ways in which the features of your offering provide benefits or added value. They explain why those features matter and how they address the buyer's challenges or requirements. Advantages are often expressed in terms of increased efficiency, cost savings, improved performance, or enhanced user experience. They help the buyer understand how your solution can solve their problems or meet their goals more effectively than competing options.

Benefits are the ultimate outcomes or results that the buyer will experience by choosing your solution. They represent the positive impact and value that your offering brings to the buyer's organization. Benefits can include increased revenue, reduced downtime, improved customer satisfaction, streamlined processes, or enhanced competitiveness. Emphasizing the benefits helps the buyer envision the positive changes and advantages they will gain by selecting your organization.

To effectively leverage features, advantages, and benefits in your bidding process, it is crucial to clearly identify and articulate them in relation to the contract requirements. This requires a deep understanding of your offering and how it aligns with the buyer's needs. It also involves effective communication skills to convey these elements in a compelling and persuasive manner.

To support individuals in mastering this skill, our team is developing an online course focused on features, advantages, and benefits in the bidding process. The course aims to provide valuable training and insights to enhance your bidding strategies and increase your chances of success. We are committed to making this course accessible to all, free of charge, as part of our mission to empower businesses and professionals in their bidding endeavors.

If you are interested in joining the course or would like more information, please reach out to us via email. We will be delighted to provide you with access and assist you in acquiring the necessary skills to effectively communicate features, advantages, and benefits in your bidding efforts.

Mastering the art of effectively communicating features, advantages, and benefits is a valuable skill that can significantly impact your bidding success. By understanding how these elements relate to the contract requirements and connect with the buyer's needs, you can craft compelling proposals that stand out from the competition.

When presenting your organization's capabilities, it is important to showcase the features that set you apart. These may include specific technologies, expertise, or resources that demonstrate your unique value proposition. By highlighting these features, you can capture the buyer's attention and differentiate yourself in the bidding process.

However, it is essential to go beyond simply listing features and delve into the advantages they provide. Advantages explain how these features translate into tangible benefits for the buyer. They demonstrate the practical value and positive impact that your offering brings to the table. By clearly articulating the advantages, you enable the buyer to see how your solution directly addresses their specific needs and challenges.

Ultimately, the benefits are what truly resonate with the buyer. These are the outcomes and results they can expect by choosing your organization. Benefits paint a compelling picture of the value they will gain from working with you. Whether it's increased efficiency, cost savings, improved productivity, or enhanced customer satisfaction, highlighting the benefits helps the buyer envision the positive impact your solution will have on their business.

To effectively utilize features, advantages, and benefits in your bidding process, it is crucial to align them with the buyer's requirements and priorities. Take the time to thoroughly understand the contract specifications and tailor your proposal to address them. By presenting your features, advantages, and benefits in a way that directly relates to the buyer's needs, you increase the chances of capturing their interest and securing the contract.

Remember, mastering the skill of effectively communicating features, advantages, and benefits takes practice and continuous improvement. It requires honing your ability to analyze and understand your offering's unique selling points and translating them into persuasive language. By investing in training and developing your communication skills, you can elevate your bidding strategy and increase your chances of success.

Communicating the unique attributes, value-added advantages, and tangible benefits of your solution positions you as a strong contender in the bidding process. So, embrace the opportunity to master this skill and unlock new possibilities for success in your bidding endeavors.

By effectively leveraging the concepts of features, advantages, and benefits in your bid proposals, you can enhance the clarity, persuasiveness, and overall impact of your messaging. Let's explore each of these elements in more detail.

Features refer to the specific characteristics and attributes of your offering. These are the tangible aspects that make your solution unique and valuable. When highlighting features, it is important to focus on those that directly align with the buyer's requirements. By clearly articulating these features, you provide the buyer with a comprehensive understanding of what your solution offers and how it can meet their needs.

Advantages go beyond features by explaining the positive impact and value they bring to the buyer. Advantages demonstrate how the features of your solution address specific pain points, overcome challenges, or deliver specific outcomes that are important to the buyer. By highlighting these advantages, you differentiate yourself from competitors and show the buyer why your solution is superior.

Benefits are the ultimate results and outcomes that the buyer will experience by choosing your solution. These are the positive changes that your solution will bring to their organization, such as increased efficiency, cost savings, improved performance, or competitive advantage. Benefits are what truly resonate with the buyer and compel them to choose your proposal over others.

To effectively utilize features, advantages, and benefits in your bid proposals, consider the following approach:

1. Understand the buyer's needs: Take the time to thoroughly analyze the buyer's requirements and understand their pain points and objectives. This will help you identify the most relevant features, advantages, and benefits to highlight in your proposal.

2. Connect features to advantages: Clearly articulate how the features of your solution translate into specific advantages for the buyer. Explain how these advantages address their needs and provide added value.

3. Emphasize the benefits: Clearly communicate the benefits that the buyer will gain by selecting your solution. Use concrete examples, metrics, or case studies to illustrate the positive impact your solution has had on previous clients or in similar contexts.

4. Tailor your messaging: Customize your bid proposal to align with the buyer's priorities. Emphasize the

features, advantages, and benefits that are most relevant and compelling to their specific situation.

5. Use clear and persuasive language: Craft your messaging in a concise, compelling, and easy-to-understand manner. Avoid technical jargon or complex terminology that may confuse the buyer. Instead, focus on communicating the value and impact of your solution in a straightforward and persuasive way.

By effectively leveraging features, advantages, and benefits in your bid proposals, you can create a compelling narrative that resonates with the buyer. This enables you to differentiate yourself from competitors, demonstrate your understanding of the buyer's needs, and showcase the value your solution brings to the table. Remember, practice and refinement are key to mastering this skill and continuously improving your bidding success.

Tailored Presentations

Presentations and interviews play a crucial role in the bidding process, complementing the written tender proposal and providing an opportunity to engage directly with the procurement team. It is important to recognize the significance of these interactions and approach them with proper preparation and a strategic mindset.

One common mistake bidders make is treating presentations or interviews as mere repetitions of the information already provided in the tender proposal. This approach fails to capitalize on the opportunity to add value and address the specific concerns and needs of the procurement team. Instead, bidders should aim to enhance the proposal with additional relevant content and demonstrate a deep understanding of the procurement team's requirements.

To excel in presentations and interviews, thorough preparation is essential. This includes practicing your delivery, refining your messaging, and familiarizing yourself with the concerns and priorities of the procurement team. Consider involving key individuals mentioned in the tender response, such as the account management team, who can contribute their expertise and establish a strong rapport with the procurement team.

During presentations or interviews, it is crucial to actively engage with the procurement team and address their concerns openly and respectfully. Do not shy away from discussing potential challenges or negative aspects, as these discussions demonstrate your preparedness and ability to mitigate risks. By acknowledging and addressing their concerns, you can build trust and show that you are a solutions-oriented bidder who values their perspective.

Indirect questions or specific scenarios related to your tender proposal can be employed to gather feedback and gain insights from the procurement team. Use this information to offer tailored solutions and demonstrate how your approach effectively addresses their concerns. Take notes during the discussion to ensure you capture all relevant points and summarize your proposed solutions. This reinforces your attentiveness and provides a basis for a follow-up discussion.

It is important to follow the instructions provided by the procurement team regarding the presentation format and time limits. Use concise and clear language, avoiding jargon or complex terminology that may confuse the audience. Focus on delivering a persuasive narrative that highlights the unique value and benefits your solution brings to the table.

Remember, presentations and interviews are an opportunity to showcase your expertise, demonstrate your understanding of the procurement team's needs, and differentiate yourself from competitors. Approach these interactions with confidence, professionalism, and a genuine commitment to addressing the concerns and delivering the best possible outcome for the procurement team.

Furthermore, it is essential to pay attention to the overall presentation style and delivery during these interactions. Your body language, tone of voice, and confidence in articulating your points can greatly influence the perception of your bid. Maintain a professional and engaging demeanor, making eye contact, using appropriate gestures, and speaking clearly and concisely.

Visual aids, such as slides or multimedia presentations, can enhance the impact of your delivery. However, it is important to strike a balance between using visuals effectively and avoiding text-heavy or cluttered slides. Focus on using visuals to support and reinforce your key messages, utilizing charts, diagrams, or graphics that simplify complex information and make it easier for the procurement team to understand.

Practice your presentation beforehand to ensure a smooth and polished delivery. Rehearse your key talking points, anticipate potential questions, and prepare concise and compelling responses. Seek feedback from colleagues or mentors to refine your presentation style and address any areas that may need improvement.

Additionally, active listening is crucial during presentations and interviews. Take the time to fully understand the questions or comments from the procurement team and respond thoughtfully. This demonstrates your attentiveness and willingness to engage in a meaningful dialogue.

Lastly, remember to leave a lasting impression by summarizing the key points of your proposal and reiterating how your solution aligns with the procurement team's objectives. Express your gratitude for the opportunity to present and emphasize your commitment to delivering value and exceeding their expectations.

By treating presentations and interviews as valuable opportunities to connect with the procurement team, demonstrate your expertise, and address their concerns, you can significantly increase your chances of success. With thorough preparation, effective communication, and a focus on delivering value, you can leave a lasting impression and stand out as a top bidder in the competitive bidding process.

In addition to the presentation itself, it is important to engage in active listening and adapt your responses based on the procurement team's feedback and reactions. Pay attention to their non-verbal cues, such as body language and facial expressions, as they can provide valuable insights into their level of interest or concerns.

During the question and answer session, be prepared to provide detailed explanations and examples to support your claims and demonstrate your expertise. Use real-world scenarios or case studies to illustrate how your solution has successfully addressed similar challenges in the past. This not only showcases your capabilities but also instills confidence in the procurement team that you have the knowledge and experience to deliver the desired outcomes.

Moreover, it is crucial to establish a rapport with the procurement team and build a relationship based on trust and credibility. Be respectful and professional in your interactions, and actively listen to their perspectives and needs. Tailor your responses to address their specific concerns and showcase how your solution can meet their unique requirements. By showing genuine interest in understanding their goals and challenges, you can establish a strong connection and differentiate yourself from other bidders.

Lastly, always follow up after the presentation or interview with a thank-you note or email. Express your appreciation for the opportunity to present and reiterate your commitment to delivering value. This small gesture demonstrates your professionalism and leaves a positive impression, reinforcing your bid and keeping you top of mind.

These opportunities allow you to showcase your organization, articulate your value proposition, and demonstrate why you are the best fit for the project. To make the most of these moments, consider the following strategies:

1. Understand the audience: Prior to the presentation or interview, thoroughly research the procurement team. Gain insights into their goals, preferences, and challenges. Tailor your content to resonate with their specific needs and expectations. Remember, a one-size-fits-all approach may not effectively engage the audience or address their concerns.

2. Develop a compelling narrative: Craft a compelling storyline that guides your presentation or interview. Start with a strong opening that captures attention and clearly articulates your unique selling proposition. Build a coherent narrative that flows logically, connecting each point to the overall theme. Use storytelling techniques and real-life examples to make your message memorable and relatable.

3. Keep it concise and focused: Time is often limited during presentations and interviews, so it is crucial to communicate your key points concisely and effectively. Avoid information overload by prioritizing the most relevant and impactful details. Use visuals, such as slides or infographics, to convey complex information in a clear and concise manner.

4. Highlight your differentiators: Clearly articulate what sets your organization apart from competitors. Emphasize your unique strengths, capabilities, and track record of success. Showcase your innovative approaches, proprietary technology, or specialized expertise that position you as the preferred choice. Align these differentiators with the specific requirements of the contract to demonstrate your relevance.

5. Engage the audience: Make your presentation or interview interactive and engaging. Encourage questions and provide thoughtful, well-structured responses. Foster a collaborative environment that allows for open dialogue and demonstrates your willingness to listen and adapt. Engage the audience by involving them in discussions, asking for their feedback, or incorporating interactive elements, if appropriate.

6. Practice and refine: Prioritize ample rehearsal time to refine your delivery and fine-tune your content. Practice in front of colleagues or mentors who can provide constructive feedback. Pay attention to your tone, body language, and pace of speech. Aim for a confident and professional demeanor that instills trust and credibility.

7. Address potential objections: Anticipate and address potential concerns or objections that the procurement team may have. Prepare well-thought-out responses to demonstrate your readiness to overcome challenges. Showcase your problem-solving skills and provide examples of how you have successfully resolved similar issues in the past.

8. Demonstrate passion and enthusiasm: Let your passion for your work shine through during the presentation or interview. Show genuine excitement about the opportunity to work on the project and convey your commitment to delivering exceptional

results. Passion and enthusiasm can be contagious, leaving a lasting impression on the procurement team.

9. Follow up and maintain relationships: After the presentation or interview, follow up with a personalized thank-you note or email. Express gratitude for the opportunity to present and reiterate your interest in the project. Use this opportunity to further reinforce key points or address any additional questions or concerns that may have arisen during the session. Building and maintaining relationships with the procurement team can open doors for future collaborations.

Presentations and interviews provide a platform for you to showcase not only your expertise but also your professionalism and ability to effectively communicate. By carefully crafting your message, engaging the audience, addressing objections, and maintaining a genuine connection, you can significantly increase your chances of securing the contract and standing out among the competition.

Streamlining

he biggest mistake in contract management is a lack of proactive engagement and communication with the buyer. This occurs when there is a failure to establish and maintain a strong working relationship, resulting in misunderstandings, misaligned expectations, and missed opportunities for collaboration and improvement.

When contract management becomes purely transactional, with minimal interaction and limited communication, it creates a disconnect between the buyer and the service provider. This lack of engagement can lead to various negative consequences, such as:

1. Misalignment of goals: Without regular communication and feedback, both parties may lose sight of the common goals and objectives. This can result in divergent paths and a failure to deliver the expected outcomes.

2. Ineffective issue resolution: If issues or concerns arise during the contract, the lack of proactive communication can hinder the timely resolution of problems. Without open dialogue, misunderstandings may escalate into larger disputes or cause delays in addressing critical issues.

3. Missed opportunities for improvement: By not actively seeking feedback and suggestions from the buyer, the service provider may miss valuable insights and opportunities for continuous improvement. Feedback is essential for identifying areas of strength and weakness and implementing necessary adjustments.

4. Lack of innovation and value-add: When there is limited engagement, the service provider may miss opportunities to introduce innovative ideas, propose value-added solutions, or suggest process enhancements. This can hinder the ability to deliver exceptional results and differentiate themselves from competitors.

5. Diminished trust and satisfaction: A lack of engagement can erode trust and satisfaction between the buyer and the service provider. Effective contract management requires building a strong relationship based on trust, transparency, and effective communication. Without this foundation, the buyer may lose confidence in the service provider's ability to meet their needs.

To avoid this mistake, it is crucial to prioritize proactive engagement and communication throughout the contract management process. This includes regular check-ins, status updates, feedback sessions, and collaborative problem-solving. By fostering open lines of communication, actively seeking input, and addressing concerns promptly, both parties can work together more effectively and achieve the desired outcomes of the contract.

Managing a contract effectively requires a structured and organized approach. It goes beyond simply delivering the scope of work; it involves building strong relationships, meeting key performance indicators (KPIs), and proactively addressing issues. By implementing clever management strategies, you can enhance your performance, exceed expectations, and strengthen your reputation with the buyer. Here are some key considerations:

1. Focus on KPIs: KPIs are essential metrics that measure the success of a contract. Collaborate with the buyer to establish clear KPIs or propose them if they are not already defined. Develop an action plan to not only meet but exceed these performance indicators. Regularly track and report progress to demonstrate your commitment to achieving outstanding results.

2. Performance reporting: Implement a systematic approach to summarizing and documenting your performance. Generate weekly or monthly reports that highlight key achievements, milestones, and progress toward meeting KPIs. These reports provide tangible evidence of your performance and serve as a basis

for continuous improvement. Use them to identify areas for optimization and cost reduction while maintaining quality.

3.   Build relationships: Once you have won a contract, invest time in building strong relationships with the buyer's teams and departments. Establish open lines of communication, actively listen to their needs, and proactively address any concerns. Understanding their expectations and working collaboratively will foster trust and pave the way for successful outcomes. This becomes particularly crucial in framework agreements where you compete with other vendors.

4.   Resolution process: Prepare a robust resolution process to address any issues or complaints that may arise during the contract period. Embrace these instances as opportunities to excel and demonstrate your ability to handle challenges. Be responsive, proactive, and focused on finding mutually beneficial solutions. Swiftly addressing and resolving issues will not only mitigate any negative impact but also showcase your professionalism and dedication to client satisfaction.

6.   Continuous improvement: Adopt a continuous improvement mindset and embrace a culture of learning. Actively seek feedback from the buyer and use it to identify areas for enhancement. Implement innovative solutions, share best practices, and explore ways to optimize processes and deliver better results. Emphasize the principles of Continuous Improvement Processes (CIP) to drive excellence and exceed expectations.

7.   Effective communication: Clear and effective communication is essential in contract management. Ensure that all stakeholders are kept well-informed about project progress, updates, and any potential changes. Regularly engage with the buyer to discuss their evolving needs and align your services

accordingly. Promptly address any questions or concerns to maintain a strong working relationship built on trust and transparency.

8. Risk management: Take a proactive approach to identify and mitigate risks throughout the contract lifecycle. Conduct thorough risk assessments to anticipate potential challenges and develop strategies to minimize their impact. Implement robust risk management processes, including contingency plans, to ensure the smooth execution of the contract and maintain uninterrupted service delivery.

9. Compliance and regulatory adherence: Stay up to date with relevant regulations, policies, and industry standards that govern the contract. Ensure strict compliance with all legal, contractual, and regulatory requirements to avoid any potential issues or penalties. Develop internal procedures and controls to monitor and maintain compliance, demonstrating your commitment to ethical practices and responsible business conduct.

10. Performance evaluation and feedback: Regularly evaluate your own performance and seek feedback from the buyer. Assess your strengths, weaknesses, and areas for improvement. Actively solicit input from the buyer on their satisfaction with your services and identify opportunities for enhancement. Use this feedback as valuable insights to refine your approach and continuously deliver exceptional results.

11. Continuous professional development: Stay ahead of industry trends, innovations, and best practices through continuous professional development. Invest in training programs, workshops, and certifications to expand your knowledge and enhance your expertise in contract management. Engage in industry forums, networking events, and knowledge-sharing platforms to stay connected and learn from peers and industry experts.

12. Leveraging technology: Embrace technology solutions that streamline contract management processes. Utilize project management tools, collaborative platforms, and document management systems to enhance efficiency, communication, and document control. Automation can help reduce manual tasks, increase accuracy, and improve overall productivity, allowing you to focus on delivering exceptional outcomes.

13. Cultivate a customer-centric approach: Above all, maintain a customer-centric mindset in all your contract management efforts. Understand the buyer's unique needs, challenges, and goals, and tailor your services to meet and exceed their expectations. Demonstrate your commitment to their success by consistently delivering value, providing exceptional service, and being responsive to their evolving requirements.

By adopting these clever management practices, you can optimize your contract management approach and position yourself as a trusted and reliable partner. Your commitment to proactive communication, risk management, compliance, continuous improvement, and customer-centricity will enhance your reputation and contribute to long-term success in contract management.

Outperforming

Seeking and embracing feedback is a mindset that sets top bidders apart from their competitors. It is not just a one-time action, but rather an ongoing commitment to personal and professional growth. The ability to actively seek and utilize feedback throughout the contract period is what enables these bidders to outperform everyone else.

One of the reasons feedback is so critical is that it provides valuable insights into your performance from the buyer's perspective. It allows you to gain a deeper understanding of their expectations, preferences, and areas where you can excel. By actively seeking feedback, you demonstrate a willingness to listen and learn, which builds trust and strengthens your relationship with the buyer.

One of the biggest mistakes bidders can make when it comes to feedback is failing to take it seriously or not utilizing it effectively. Feedback is a valuable resource that provides valuable insights into the strengths and weaknesses of your bid. Ignoring or dismissing feedback can hinder your growth and limit your chances of success in future bids.

One common mistake is not actively seeking feedback. Some bidders may feel hesitant or fearful about asking for feedback, fearing it will reveal shortcomings or reflect poorly on their abilities. However, this approach denies them the opportunity to learn and improve. By not actively seeking feedback, bidders miss out on valuable insights that could help them refine their approach and enhance their future bids.

Another mistake is not using feedback strategically. Feedback should not be seen as a one-time evaluation but as an ongoing process of improvement. Bidders should analyze the feedback they receive and identify recurring patterns or areas for improvement. Simply collecting feedback without taking the necessary steps to implement changes or address weaknesses limits its potential impact.

Additionally, disregarding feedback from the buyer or procurement team can be a detrimental mistake. Their feedback represents the perspective of the decision-makers and provides valuable insights into their expectations and preferences. Dismissing or downplaying their feedback can lead to missed opportunities to align your bid more effectively with their needs and increase your chances of success.

Furthermore, not sharing feedback within the organization is another mistake. Feedback should be seen as a collective learning opportunity. By sharing feedback with your team, you can collaborate on addressing identified weaknesses and developing strategies for improvement. Failing to share feedback internally limits the potential for collective growth and improvement.

To overcome these mistakes, bidders should approach feedback with an open mind and a growth mindset. Actively seek feedback, listen attentively, and reflect on the insights provided. Use feedback strategically to identify areas for improvement and develop action plans to address them. Share feedback within your organization to foster a culture of continuous improvement.

So, feedback helps you identify areas for improvement and refine your strategies. It shines a light on any weaknesses or gaps in your approach, allowing you to take corrective measures and enhance your performance. Without feedback, it is challenging to gauge the effectiveness of your actions and make informed decisions for future bids.

Top bidders understand that feedback is not just limited to the buyer's evaluation. They proactively seek feedback from their own team members, colleagues, and industry experts. This comprehensive approach allows them to gather diverse perspectives and gain a well-rounded view of their performance. They value constructive criticism and use it as fuel to drive their continuous improvement efforts.

Furthermore, feedback provides an opportunity for self-reflection and self-assessment. It allows you to objectively evaluate your strengths and weaknesses, enabling you to leverage your strengths and address any areas that require development. By embracing feedback, you can unlock your full potential and become the best version of yourself as a bidder.

To fully harness the power of feedback, it is important to create a culture that encourages open communication and feedback exchange within your organization. Foster an environment where team members feel comfortable sharing their observations, insights, and suggestions. Encourage peer feedback and collaboration to drive collective growth and learning.

In addition to the intrinsic benefits of feedback, there are several specific strategies that top bidders employ to maximize its impact and use it as a catalyst for their success.

Firstly, top bidders actively request feedback from the buyer or procurement team after each bid, regardless of the outcome. They understand that feedback is not only valuable for improving their future bids but also for strengthening their relationship with the buyer. They approach the feedback process with a genuine desire to learn and grow, demonstrating their commitment to excellence.

Secondly, top bidders go beyond the generic feedback and seek specific, actionable insights. They ask targeted questions to understand the strengths and weaknesses of their proposal, presentation, and overall approach. This helps them identify areas where they excelled and capitalize on those strengths in future bids. It also allows them to address any shortcomings and refine their strategies for continuous improvement.

Furthermore, top bidders take feedback seriously by implementing the necessary changes based on the received insights. They view feedback as a roadmap for enhancement and innovation. By incorporating the feedback into their bidding processes, they ensure that they are continuously evolving and staying ahead of the competition.

Another key aspect of leveraging feedback is sharing the lessons learned within their organization. Top bidders understand that feedback is not only valuable for individual growth but also for the collective improvement of their team.

They conduct internal debriefings and knowledge-sharing sessions to disseminate the feedback and ensure that everyone benefits from the insights gained.

Moreover, top bidders proactively seek feedback from their peers, mentors, and industry experts. They participate in networking events, attend conferences, and engage in professional communities to gather diverse perspectives and learn from the experiences of others. By seeking external feedback, they expand their knowledge base and gain valuable insights into industry best practices.

Ultimately, the ability to outperform everyone in the bidding process hinges on your willingness to seek, embrace, and act upon feedback. By integrating feedback into your bidding strategy and making it an integral part of your growth mindset, you position yourself as a bidder who is constantly evolving, improving, and exceeding expectations.

Be proactive in seeking feedback, listen attentively, and take action to implement the insights gained. With a commitment to continuous improvement fueled by feedback, you can consistently outperform others and achieve greater success in your bidding endeavors.

Seeking and embracing feedback is a vital component of outperforming everyone in the bidding process. It enables you to gain valuable insights, refine your strategies, and continuously improve your performance. By making feedback an integral part of your bidding approach, you can stay ahead of the competition, exceed expectations, and position yourself as a trusted and successful bidder.

Simple Mindedness

One of the most significant mistakes that bidding organizations make after winning a contract is shifting their focus solely on fulfilling the order while neglecting the needs and expectations of the client. This common error often leads to the loss of contracts and missed opportunities for long-term success.

Here are a few reasons why this shift in focus is detrimental:

1. Client satisfaction and retention: Neglecting the needs and expectations of the client can result in dissatisfaction and disappointment. If clients feel that their requirements are not being met or their expectations are not being considered, they may become dissatisfied with the services provided. This dissatisfaction can lead to strained relationships, loss of trust, and ultimately, client attrition. By prioritizing the client's needs and expectations, organizations can foster client satisfaction, strengthen relationships, and increase client retention.

2. Missed opportunities for upselling and cross-selling: When organizations solely focus on fulfilling the immediate order, they miss out on potential opportunities for upselling and cross-selling. By understanding the client's needs and expectations beyond the current contract, organizations can identify additional products or services that may be beneficial to the client. By proactively presenting these offerings, organizations can increase revenue and enhance the client's overall experience.

3. Reputation and referrals: Neglecting the client's needs and expectations can harm an organization's reputation. Dissatisfied clients may share their negative experiences with others, tarnishing the organization's image and potentially deterring future clients. On the other hand, organizations that prioritize client satisfaction and consistently deliver exceptional service are more likely to receive positive referrals

and recommendations, enhancing their reputation and attracting new business opportunities.

4. Competitive advantage: Organizations that prioritize the client's needs and expectations differentiate themselves from competitors. By providing tailored solutions and going above and beyond to meet client requirements, organizations stand out in a crowded marketplace. This customer-centric approach can give them a competitive edge, helping them win repeat business and secure new contracts.

5. Long-term partnerships: Neglecting the client's needs and expectations hinders the development of long-term partnerships. Clients are more likely to partner with organizations that understand their unique requirements, actively listen to their feedback, and consistently deliver exceptional service. By prioritizing the client's needs and expectations, organizations can foster trust, collaboration, and mutual growth, paving the way for long-term and mutually beneficial partnerships.

Winning a tender is just the beginning of the customer journey, and it is crucial to deliver an exceptional client experience throughout the entire contract period. To ensure client satisfaction, our team emphasizes the development of a comprehensive customer experience management plan. This plan focuses on understanding and addressing the client's unique requirements, preferences, and challenges.

It is important to recognize that managing an order or enquiry is about more than just delivering a product or solution. It is about creating a positive and memorable experience for the client and all stakeholders involved. Each interaction and touchpoint should leave a lasting impression that reflects your commitment to their success.

I vividly recall a situation where an organization lost a contract due to their lack of attentiveness and support towards their client. Despite receiving regular orders and enquiries, they failed to handle requests for items not available in their inventory. Instead of proactively seeking alternative solutions or collaborating with third-party suppliers, they simply declined to provide a quote, leaving the client disappointed and seeking alternative options. A more client-focused approach would have involved identifying reliable partners or sub-contractors to fulfill these specific orders while meeting all contract requirements. This proactive and collaborative approach not only ensures client satisfaction but also helps to build strong partnerships and expand capabilities.

In the realm of client management, it is essential to prioritize the client's needs and go the extra mile to meet and exceed their expectations. By establishing a service environment that values client satisfaction, you not only save time but also create opportunities for continuous improvement. Each successful project becomes a valuable addition to your portfolio, providing you with case studies and evidence of your expertise for future tender proposals.

Remember, in the bidding world, the client reigns supreme. It is our responsibility to serve them diligently, nurture strong relationships, and consistently deliver exceptional results. By adopting a client-focused approach and continuously improving our services, we position ourselves for long-term success and future contract wins.

Spending

The of the biggest mistakes that vendors can make when trying to increase spending within a contract is failing to actively engage with the buyer and understand their evolving needs and priorities. This can occur due to several reasons:

1. Lack of Communication: Vendors may assume that winning the contract means their work is done and overlook the importance of ongoing communication with the buyer. They may fail to reach out to procurement teams or other relevant staff members within the buying organization who may have additional needs or new projects. This lack of communication prevents vendors from uncovering opportunities for expansion and limits their chances of increasing spending.

2. Neglecting Relationship Building: Building strong relationships with the buyer is essential for long-term success. However, some vendors may focus solely on transactional interactions rather than investing time and effort into cultivating meaningful connections. By failing to establish rapport and understand the buyer's goals and objectives, vendors miss out on valuable insights and may struggle to align their offerings with the buyer's evolving requirements.

3. Lack of Proactive Approach: Vendors who adopt a passive approach and simply fulfill the contractual obligations without going the extra mile miss out on opportunities to introduce new solutions or demonstrate innovative products or materials. By not actively seeking ways to add value or propose new ideas, vendors limit their potential for upselling and fail to capitalize on opportunities to increase spending within the contract.

4. Failure to Review and Adapt: Contracts should not be treated as static agreements. Vendors who neglect to regularly review the contract's terms and conditions, performance metrics, and deliverables miss the

chance to identify areas for improvement or propose modifications. Without this proactive evaluation, vendors may fail to recognize opportunities for expanding the scope of the contract or suggesting new services that could generate additional revenue.

5. Inability to Anticipate Future Needs: Winning a contract should be seen as an entry point into understanding the buyer's long-term plans. However, vendors who do not actively seek insights into the buyer's strategic direction and upcoming initiatives may miss out on opportunities to align their offerings with future needs. Failing to anticipate and position themselves to address these needs hinders vendors from maximizing spending within the contract.

The biggest mistake vendors can make when trying to increase spending within a contract is a lack of proactive engagement, failure to communicate and build relationships with the buyer, and a failure to adapt to changing circumstances. By avoiding these mistakes and adopting a proactive and customer-centric approach, vendors can significantly enhance their chances of expanding the scope of the contract and increasing spending.

Maximizing the potential of a contract goes beyond the initial scope outlined during the tender process. Many bidders overlook the fact that winning a contract does not necessarily limit the buyer's purchasing power. This principle applies to frameworks as well, yet it remains largely unknown to many prospective vendors.

To truly capitalize on a contract, bidders should actively engage with the procurement teams and other relevant stakeholders within the buying organization. By establishing communication channels and fostering relationships, vendors can uncover additional needs or upcoming projects that may require their products or services. Winning a contract should be seen as an opportunity to delve deeper into the buyer's future plans and align their offerings accordingly.

Moreover, vendors should seize the chance to showcase new solutions they have developed or demonstrate the capabilities of their latest products or materials. By presenting innovative ideas and highlighting the value they can bring, vendors can not only enhance their chances of increasing spending within the existing contract but also open doors for new opportunities.

Contracts should serve as stepping stones to continuous growth and expansion. Vendors should have well-defined processes in place to proactively identify opportunities for upselling, cross-selling, and introducing new products or solutions. Regularly reviewing and revisiting the contract's terms and conditions can help identify areas where additional value can be provided or new offerings can be introduced.

Winning a contract is not the endpoint but rather the beginning of a journey towards increasing spending and forging stronger relationships with buyers. By going the extra mile to understand the buyer's long-term plans, presenting innovative solutions, and consistently seeking opportunities to expand the scope of the contract, vendors can maximize their potential and achieve sustainable growth in a dynamic market.

Here are some key strategies to consider:

1. Cultivate Relationships: Building strong relationships with the procurement teams and relevant stakeholders within the buying organization is crucial. Regular communication, meetings, and networking events can help foster trust and establish a deeper understanding of the buyer's needs. By proactively engaging with these individuals, vendors can position themselves as trusted advisors and increase the likelihood of being considered for additional projects or requirements.

2. Understand the Buyer's Future Plans: Winning a contract provides a unique vantage point to gain insights into the buyer's long-term objectives. Vendors should leverage this opportunity to delve deeper into the buyer's strategic direction and identify upcoming initiatives or expansions. By aligning their offerings with the buyer's future plans, vendors can position themselves as valuable partners who can contribute

to the buyer's success and increase the likelihood of additional spending.

3. Present New Solutions and Innovations: In a dynamic market, buyers are constantly seeking innovative solutions that can address their evolving challenges. Vendors should proactively showcase their latest products, technologies, or services that can bring added value to the buyer's operations. Demonstrating how these new solutions can solve existing pain points or improve efficiency can be a compelling way to expand the scope of the contract and increase spending.

4. Conduct Regular Reviews: Contracts should not be treated as static documents but rather as living agreements that can be reviewed and optimized over time. Vendors should establish a process to regularly evaluate the contract's terms and conditions, performance metrics, and key deliverables. This review process provides an opportunity to identify areas for improvement, propose modifications, or suggest new services that can generate additional revenue.

5. Offer Value-Added Services: Beyond the core deliverables outlined in the contract, vendors can explore opportunities to provide value-added services that align with the buyer's needs. This can include offering training programs, ongoing support, maintenance services, or consulting expertise. By demonstrating a commitment to the buyer's success and providing comprehensive solutions, vendors can increase customer satisfaction and create a pathway for increased spending.

6. Stay Agile and Responsive: Markets and business environments can change rapidly, and vendors need to be adaptable to capitalize on emerging opportunities. Keeping a finger on the pulse of industry trends, regulatory changes, and market dynamics allows vendors to identify potential areas for

expansion within existing contracts. Being proactive in identifying these opportunities and swiftly responding to buyer requirements positions vendors as agile partners who can cater to evolving needs.

Increasing spending within a contract requires proactive engagement, understanding of the buyer's future plans, and a commitment to delivering value. By cultivating relationships, presenting new solutions, conducting regular reviews, offering value-added services, and staying agile, vendors can optimize their contracts and unlock the full potential for growth and expansion.

Unlock Free Bid Guidance

Are you grappling with the steep costs of retaining full-time bid managers, and looking for an affordable, yet high-quality alternative? I can wholeheartedly recommend a company that revolutionized my bidding strategy: Bid Champions.

Bid Champions is renowned for offering top-tier bid management support without the hefty price tag that's usually attached to it. Their team of specialists impressed me with their skill in delivering superior bid management services, equipping my business with the tools needed to boost the odds of winning significant contracts.

What sets Bid Champions apart for me is their genuine commitment to the business community. Besides their competitively priced services, they regularly organize free training sessions and even shoulder the responsibility of one tender each month, free of charge, for a company they believe deserves that break. Their mission to support businesses in the demanding bidding landscape is truly commendable.

Here's some good news: Bid Champions has extended an offer to share their expertise and provide free guidance or bid advice for your current tender proposal.

If you're interested in exploring this unique offer, all you need to do is send an email to win@bidchampions.com, with "Worst Bidding Mistakes" as the subject.

Share some of the challenges or mistakes you've encountered in your bidding process. The Bid Champions team will carefully review all submissions and choose a company they believe could truly benefit from their guidance.

This could be a game-changer for your bidding efforts. From my experience, I can say that the support provided by Bid Champions can indeed propel your bidding success. Don't hesitate to reach out to them; it could transform your approach to bidding and set your business on a path to significant growth.

Having Fun

Ever wondered what it's like to be part of a team that genuinely invests in your growth and development? I found this and much more when I joined Bid Champions. This organization is truly committed to helping every team member discover and fulfil their true potential. I've seen firsthand how they've transformed bidders into industry leaders.

What stood out to me about Bid Champions was their recognition that each individual brings their unique talents and expertise. I was pleasantly surprised to find that their training and Continuous Professional Development (CPD) programs are not one-size-fits-all but customized to align with my specific talents and career aspirations. Whether you join as an employee or an independent consultant, working under the Bid Champions umbrella is not just a job—it's a thrilling and enriching journey of constant learning and growth.

Their training programs are comprehensive, covering everything from bid management best practices and effective communication strategies to negotiation skills, market analysis, and the latest industry trends. The hands-on training and mentorship I received enabled me to gain practical experience and hone my skills in real-time.

What really sets Bid Champions apart is their emphasis on ongoing professional development. With the bidding landscape continuously evolving, staying ahead of the curve is crucial. Through regular CPD initiatives—workshops, webinars, conferences, and networking events—Bid Champions ensures their bidders are always equipped with the latest techniques, tools, and strategies.

Being a part of the Bid Champions team is not just about the work—it's about being part of a supportive and collaborative community. The environment is ripe for continuous learning, and innovation and creativity are encouraged. The passion and engagement I observed in my peers were palpable, resulting in remarkable results for the clients we served.

So, if you're looking to embark on a fulfilling journey in the bidding industry, I can wholeheartedly recommend joining the team at Bid Champions. This could be your chance to unlock your true potential and make your career in bidding a truly rewarding and enjoyable experience.

You can find out more about these exciting opportunities by reaching out at win@bidchampions.com. Trust me, it could be the best decision you make for your career.